Plays from Dickens

Plays from Dickens

by

MICHAEL & MOLLIE HARDWICK

JOHN MURRAY

Fifty Albemarle Street London

'Bardell *v.* Pickwick' is fully protected by copy-
right and no performance may be given without
a licence from

The League of Dramatists,
84 Drayton Gardens,
London, S.W.10

from whose Secretary all information about fees
can be obtained.

Printed in Great Britain by
Cox & Wyman Ltd., London, Reading
and Fakenham

0 7195 2016 9

FOREWORD

A set of Charles Dickens's works – over twenty fat volumes – makes a formidable array on any bookshelf. Any one of those volumes, opened at random, might offer a daunting prospect of very full pages in which long descriptive passages seem frequently to occur, with every so often a somewhat grotesque illustration showing characters so exaggerated in features and pose that they seem too absurd to believe in.

Yet, almost everyone who has read Dickens knows that this forbidding impression is a totally wrong one: that, of all writers, he has the most sheer fascination to offer, whether in terms of hilarious comedy, or stark drama, or moving sympathy for life's victims. Some readers discover this too late, and regret the years of pleasure they have missed. The time to approach Dickens is in youth, for there is so much of his work, and much that is so compelling, that he may be returned to again and again, always guaranteeing refreshment when other reading or experience palls. As with many pleasures, though, a little initial effort is called for. It is easier not to read a long book than to do so; but, with Dickens, just take the plunge and you will find the currents of his genius bearing you along the rest of the way.

It seems to us that one of the best ways of making that start is by way of drama. Dramatizations of Dickens's works, presented on television, film, radio and the stage, have brought many people their first realization of what he has to offer. All his life he loved acting and presenting plays, and the solo readings he gave of his works for many years were remarkable performances of moving and even terrifying intensity, taking such toll of his powers that they helped to kill him in his fifties. His theatrical sense is constantly evident in his story-writing, and if some of his characters, like the illustrations, seem a bit removed from reality, it is partly because he saw them like figures on a stage, whose performances reflect real life but do not exactly copy it.

So we have written this book of dramatizations with the idea of making the classroom Dickens's theatre for a few short scenes, showing him in several of his moods, which will give those who take part and those who merely listen something of the 'feel' of Dickens. We have taken the usual adapter's licence in translating what was meant to be read into what is speakable, and have used Charles Dickens himself as a narrator, introducing each episode. The playlets can be either acted or read. We include a minimum of directions and suggest that through these pieces pupils might learn, by trial and error, some of the rudiments of acting and producing.

The longer play, *Bardell* v. *Pickwick*, is intended both for classroom use and for full-scale performance on the stage (see the introductory note on page 49). If anything can convince anybody that Dickens is worth reading, this immensely funny episode, with its cast of unforgettable characters, should most surely do the trick, though we hope that the short pieces will have their effect, too. One thing is certain: those whose appetite for reading Dickens does become whetted will have a lifetime's enjoyment before them.

MICHAEL & MOLLIE HARDWICK

CONTENTS

NICHOLAS TURNS THE TABLES

From *Nicholas Nickleby*

Characters:

Charles Dickens	Cobbey
Squeers	Graymarsh
Nicholas Nickleby	A Boy
Mrs. Squeers	Second Boy
Smike	Third Boy
Head Boy	Tompkins
Bolder	Other Boys

DICKENS: Although any man who had proved his unfitness
for any other occupation in life was once free, without
examination or qualification, to open a school anywhere;
and although schoolmasters, as a race, were the block-
heads and impostors who might naturally be expected
to spring from such a state of things, the masters of the
Yorkshire schools were the lowest and most rotten of
them all. I was always curious about the Yorkshire
schools, and resolved to write about them. I went down
into Yorkshire in the guise of the friend of a poor
widowed lady who didn't know what to do with the little
boy with whom she had been left, and had thought of
sending him to a Yorkshire school. The Mr. Squeers
whom I am about to present to you is but a mildly drawn
representative of a class of men responsible for inflicting

upon unwanted children such treatment, involving neglect, cruelty and disease, as no writer of fiction of my time would have had the boldness to invent. Nicholas Nickleby, a young man from London, has innocently joined the staff of Dotheboys Hall, of which Squeers is headmaster. It is the depth of winter as Nicholas is awakened on the morning after his long, cold, uncomfortable coach journey to Yorkshire.

SQUEERS: Nickleby! Nickleby! Past seven, Nickleby!

NICHOLAS (*waking*): Eh! What? Oh, Mr. Squeers.

SQUEERS: Past seven, Nickleby.

NICHOLAS: Has morning come already?

SQUEERS: Ay, that it has. And ready iced, too. Now, come on. Tumble up, will you?

NICHOLAS: I won't be many minutes, sir. As soon as I've had my wash ...

SQUEERS: Wash! You can't wash this morning.

NICHOLAS: Not wash myself?

SQUEERS: The pump's froze. You'll have to make do with a dry polish, till we break the ice in the well and get a bucket up for the boys. Now, don't stand staring at me. Look sharp, will you?

MRS. SQUEERS: Squeery!

SQUEERS: Here's Mrs. Squeers. Come in, my love.

NICHOLAS: Good morning, ma'am.

MRS. SQUEERS: Drat it, I can't find the school spoon anywhere.

SQUEERS: Why, never mind that, my dear. It's of no consequence.

MRS. SQUEERS: No consequence! Why how you talk! Isn't it brimstone morning?

SQUEERS: Ah, I forgot, my dear. Yes, it certainly is. We purify the boys' bloods now and then, Nickleby.

MRS. SQUEERS: Purify fiddlesticks' ends! Don't think, young man, we go to the expense of flower of brimstone and molasses just to purify them. Because if you think we carry on the business in that way, you're mistaken, I'll tell you plain.

SQUEERS (*warningly*): My dear!

MRS. SQUEERS: Oh, nonsense! If the young man comes to be a teacher here, let him understand at once that we want no foolery about those boys. They have the brimstone and treacle, partly because if they hadn't something or other in the way of medicine they'd be always ailing and giving a world of trouble, and partly because it spoils their appetites and comes cheaper than breakfast and dinner. So it does them good and us good at the same time – and that's fair enough, I'm sure. Ah, here it is all the time. Now, hurry along, will you?

SQUEERS: Coming at once, my dear. Ah, Nickleby, a most invaluable woman, that.

NICHOLAS: Indeed, sir.

SQUEERS: I don't know her equal. I do not know her equal. That woman, Nickleby, is always the same – always the same bustling, lively, active, saving creetur that you see her now.

NICHOLAS: I'm sure, sir.

SQUEERS: I always say, when I'm up in London, that to them boys she is a mother. But she is more than a mother to them: ten times more. She does things for them boys, Nickleby, that I don't believe half the mothers going would do for their own sons.

NICHOLAS: I should think they wouldn't, sir.

SQUEERS: But come. Let's go to the schoolroom.

DICKENS: Picking up his cane, Squeers led the way through the darkness, across the frozen yard, to a door in the rear of the house.

SQUEERS (*proudly*): There, Nickleby – this is our shop!

DICKENS: Nicholas stared about him. By degrees, the place resolved itself into a bare and dirty room, with a couple of windows, whereof a tenth part might be of glass, the remainder being stopped up with old copybooks and paper. There were a couple of long, old, rickety desks, cut and notched and inked and damaged in every possible way, two or three benches for the pupils and a desk for Squeers.

But the pupils! Pale and haggard faces; lank and bony figures; children with the countenances of old men. There were little faces which should have been handsome, darkened with the scowl of sullen, dogged sufferings; there was childhood with the light of its eye quenched, its beauty gone, and its helplessness alone remaining. With every kindly sympathy and affection blasted in its birth, with every young and healthy feeling flogged and starved down, with every revengeful passion that can fester in swollen hearts eating its evil way to their core in silence, what an incipient Hell was breeding here!

SQUEERS (*rapping the desk with his cane*): Now, Mrs. Squeers. Is that physicking over?

MRS. SQUEERS: Just over. Here, Smike!

SMIKE (*cringing*): Yes, ma'am?

MRS. SQUEERS: Take this bowl away. And look sharp now!

SMIKE: Yes ma'am.

[MRS. SQUEERS *and* SMIKE *leave*]

SQUEERS (*rapping with his cane*): Let any boy speak a word without leave, and I'll take the skin off his back. Now, boys, I've been to London, and have returned to my family and you, as strong and well as ever.

HEAD BOY: Three cheers for Mr. Squeers.

[*The* BOYS *cheer feebly and without meaning it*]

SQUEERS: I have seen the parents of some boys, and they're so glad to hear how their sons are getting on that there's no prospect at all of their taking them away, which of course is a very pleasant thing for all parties to reflect upon.

[One or two boys cry silently at this news]

I have had disappointments to contend against. Bolder's father was two pound ten short. Bolder!

BOLDER: Yes, sir.

SQUEERS: You'll see me presently.

[He flourishes the cane]

BOLDER: Yes, sir.

SQUEERS: Now, let's see. Ah, there's a letter for Cobbey. Stand up, Cobbey.

COBBEY *(standing)*: Sir?

SQUEERS: Cobbey's grandmother is dead, and his Uncle John has took to drinking, which is all the news his sister sends, except eighteenpence, which will just pay for that broken square of glass. Sit down, Cobbey.

[COBBEY sits and buries his head in his hands]

Graymarsh!

GRAYMARSH *(standing)*: Sir?

SQUEERS: Graymarsh's maternal aunt is very glad to hear he's so well and happy, and sends her respectful compliments to Mrs. Squeers, and thinks she must be an angel. She likewise thinks Mr. Squeers is too good for this world, but hopes he may long be spared to carry on the business. Tells Graymarsh to study everything to please Mr. and Mrs. Squeers, and look upon them as his only friends; and that Graymarsh will not object to sleeping five in a bed, which no Christian should. Ah, a delightful letter! Very affecting indeed. Graymarsh, sit down.

[GRAYMARSH sits]

SQUEERS: Mobbs.

[MOBBS stands]

Mobbs' stepmother took to her bed on hearing that he wouldn't eat fat and has been very ill ever since. She

wishes to know, by an early post, where he expects to go
if he quarrels with his vittles, and with what feelings he
could turn up his nose at the cow's liver broth after his
good master had asked a blessing on it. This was told
her in the London newspapers – not by Mr. Squeers,
for he is too kind and too good to set anybody against
anybody. She is sorry to find Mobbs is discontented,
which is sinful and horrid, and hopes Mr. Squeers will
flog him into a happier state of mind. With this view,
she has also stopped his halfpenny a week pocket money.
Sit down, Mobbs, because later you mayn't be able.
And now, Bolder.

BOLDER (*standing*): Sir?

SQUEERS: Come here, Bolder.

> [BOLDER *comes out.* SQUEERS *seizes one of his
> hands and raises the cane, but pauses to peer at the
> hand*]

What's this, eh?

BOLDER: Sir?

> [SQUEERS *gives him a cut with the cane*]

SQUEERS: That on your hand. What do you call that, eh?

BOLDER: I ... I think it's a wart, sir.

SQUEERS: A wart it certainly is, Bolder.

BOLDER: Please, sir, I can't help it, indeed, sir. They *will*
come. It's the dirty work, I think, sir. And the pump's
frozen.

NICHOLAS: That's true, Mr. Squeers.

SQUEERS: You wait till you're asked, Nickleby. Now,
Bolder, you're an incorrigible young scoundrel, and as
the last thrashing did you no good we must see what
another will do.

> [*He gives* BOLDER *several cuts across the hand,
> causing him to double up in pain.* NICHOLAS *steps
> forward, as if to intervene, but does not.* SQUEERS
> *pushes* BOLDER *away*]

SMIKE (*standing up*): Please, sir.

SQUEERS: Eh? Oh, it's you, is it, Smike?

SMIKE: Yes, sir. Please, sir, is there . . .

SQUEERS: Well?

SMIKE: Have you . . . did anybody . . .

SQUEERS: Out with it!

SMIKE: Has nothing been heard about me, sir?

SQUEERS: Devil a bit! Not a word, and never will be. Now, this is a pretty sort of thing, isn't it, that you should have been left here all these years and no money paid after the first six, nor no clue to be got who you belong to? It's a pretty sort of thing that I should have to feed a great fellow like you, and never hope to get one penny for it, isn't it? A pretty sort of thing. Come out here.

> [SMIKE *comes out.* SQUEERS *raises the cane and* SMIKE *obediently puts up his hand.* NICHOLAS *steps forward*]

NICHOLAS: Mr. Squeers . . .!

SQUEERS: Yes, Nickleby?

NICHOLAS: I . . . Nothing, sir.

SQUEERS: Thank you, Nickleby.

> [*He canes* SMIKE, *then pushes him away*]

Now, then – first class out!

> [*a few boys shuffle out and stand in a row before him*]

This is the first class in English spelling and philosophy, Nickleby. Now, then, where's the first boy?

A BOY: Please, sir, he's cleaning the back parlour window.

SQUEERS: So he is, to be sure. We go upon the practical mode of teaching, Nickleby; the regular education system. C-l-e-a-n, clean, verb active, to make bright, to scour. W-i-n, win, d-e-r, winder, a casement. When the boy knows this out of the book he goes and does it. Where's the next boy?

SECOND BOY: Please, sir, he's weeding the garden.

SQUEERS: To be sure. So he is. B-o-t, bot, t-i-n, tin, bottin, n-e-y, ney, bottiney, noun substantive, a knowledge of plants. When he has learned that bottiney means a knowledge of plants he goes and knows 'em. That's our system, Nickleby. What do you think of it?

NICHOLAS (*sarcastically*): It's a very *useful* one, at any rate.

SQUEERS: Quite so. Third boy, what's a horse?

THIRD BOY: A beast, sir.

SQUEERS: So it is. Ain't it, Nickleby?

NICHOLAS: I believe there is no doubt of that, sir.

SQUEERS: Of course there isn't. A horse is a quadruped, and a quadruped's Latin for beast, as everybody that's gone through the grammar knows, or else where's the use of having grammars at all?

NICHOLAS: Where indeed?

SQUEERS: As you're perfect in that, boy, go and look after *my* horse. And rub him down well, or I'll rub you down. The rest of the class, go and draw water up till somebody tells you to leave off. It's washing day tomorrow and they'll want the coppers filled.

DICKENS: The cruelty of which he had been an unwilling witness, the behaviour of Squeers, the filthy place, the sights and sounds about him, all contributed towards a feeling in Nicholas of depression. During the next few weeks he did what little he could to ease the lot of his wretched charges, especially that of the pathetic Smike, who, seeing Nicholas as his only friend in the world, took to following him to and fro and serving him in every way he could. This association was soon recognized by the Squeers and added to other growing resentments against Nicholas, with the result that upon poor Smike all the spleen and ill-humour that could not be vented on Nicholas were unceasingly bestowed. On one cold January morning, Nicholas awoke to find Smike missing from his place in the wretched dormitory.

sQUEERS: Are you going to sleep all day up there?

MRS. SQUEERS: Lazy hounds!

NICKLEBY: We shall be down directly, sir. Come along, boys.

[*The* BOYS *groan and mumble with cold*]

SQUEERS: Down directly? You'd better be, or I'll be down on some of you in less. Where's that Smike?

MRS. SQUEERS: Do you hear, Smike? Do you want your head broke in a fresh place?

SQUEERS: Send that obstinate scoundrel down, Nickleby.

NICHOLAS: He is not here, sir.

SQUEERS: Don't lie to me, sir!

NICHOLAS: I tell you he is *not* here, sir.

MRS. SQUEERS: Then where have you hid him? We know you've been making a favourite of him and spoiling him.

NICHOLAS: For aught I know he is at the bottom of the nearest pond. I have not seen him since last night.

SQUEERS: Confound you, Nickleby! Boys, which of you knows anything about this?

TOMPKINS: Please, sir, I think Smike's run away, sir.

SQUEERS: Ha! Who said that?

BOYS: Tompkins, sir.

SQUEERS: Come here, Tompkins.

[TOMPKINS *comes cringing forward.* SQUEERS *seizes him*]

You think he has run away, do you?

TOMPKINS: Yes, please, sir.

SQUEERS: And what, sir, what reason have you to suppose that any boy would want to run away from this establishment? Eh?

[TOMPKINS *begins to cry.* SQUEERS *shakes him violently and flings him back amongst the boys*]

If any other boy thinks Smike has run away I should be glad to have a talk with him. As to you, Nickleby, you think he has run away, I suppose?

NICHOLAS: I think it extremely likely.

MRS. SQUEERS: He didn't tell you he was going, I suppose.

NICHOLAS: He did not. I am very glad he did not, for it would then have been my duty to warn you.

SQUEERS: Which no doubt you would have been devilish sorry to do.

NICHOLAS: You interpret my feelings with great accuracy.

MRS. SQUEERS: What on earth are you a-talking to him for Squeery? If you get a parcel of proud-stomached teachers that set the young dogs a-rebelling, what else can you look for? Now, you boys, take pattern by Smike if you dare. See what he'll get for himself when he is brought back.

SQUEERS: If I catch him I'll only stop short of flaying him alive.

MRS. SQUEERS: *If* you catch him! You can't help it, if you go the right way to work. He must have gone the York way, and by a public road, too.

SQUEERS: Why must he?

MRS. SQUEERS: Stupid! He never had any money, had he?

SQUEERS: Never had a penny of his own in his whole life that I know of.

MRS. SQUEERS: To be sure. And he didn't take anything to eat with him, that *I'll* answer for. So he must beg his way, and he could do that nowhere but on the public road.

SQUEERS: That's true, my dear.

MRS. SQUEERS: Yes, but you would never have thought of it, for all that. Now if you take the chaise and go one road, and I borrow Swallow's chaise and go the other, what with keeping our eyes open, and asking questions, one or other of us is pretty certain to lay hold of him.

DICKENS: The worthy lady's plan was adopted. Nicholas remained behind, in a tumult of feeling. Death from want and exposure to the weather was the best that could be expected from the protracted wandering of so poor and helpless a creature. There was little perhaps to choose between this fate and a return to the tender mercies of the school. In the evening of the next day, Squeers returned alone.

SQUEERS: No news of the scamp! I'll have consolation for this out of somebody, Nickleby, if Mrs. Squeers don't hunt him down – so I give you warning.

NICHOLAS: It is not in my power to console you, sir.

SQUEERS: Isn't it? We shall see. None of your whining here, Mr. Puppy!

[A commotion of boys outside]

MRS. SQUEERS: Lift him out. Bring him in. Take care ...
[SMIKE, half-collapsing, is brought in]

SQUEERS: Ah! Well done, my dear, well done! Now, is every boy here?

BOYS: Yes, sir.

SQUEERS: Each boy to his place, then. Nickleby – to your desk, sir.

[The BOYS form up. SQUEERS seizes SMIKE by the collar and forces him to his knees]

Have you anything to say for yourself, Smike?
[SMIKE cannot answer]

Have you anything to say? No?
[He seizes his cane]

Nothing I suppose. Stand a little out of the way, Mrs. Squeers, my dear. I've hardly got room enough.

SMIKE: Spare me, sir!

SQUEERS: Oh, that's all, is it? Yes, I'll flog you within an inch of your life, and spare you that.

MRS. SQUEERS (*laughing*): That's a good 'un!

SMIKE: I was driven to do it.

SQUEERS: Driven to do it, were you? Oh, it wasn't your fault; it was mine, I suppose.

MRS. SQUEERS: A nasty ungrateful, pig-headed, brutish,

     obstinate, sneaking dog. What does he mean by that?

SQUEERS: Stand aside, my dear. We'll try and find out.

[He raises his cane. NICHOLAS *steps forward]*

NICHOLAS: Stop!

SQUEERS: Who cried stop?

NICHOLAS: I. This must not go on.

*[*SQUEERS, *astonished, lets go of* SMIKE]*

SQUEERS: Must not go on!

NICHOLAS: It shall not. I will prevent it. You have dis-regarded all my quiet interference on the miserable lad's behalf. Don't blame me for this public interference. You have brought it on yourself.

SQUEERS: Sit down, beggar!

[He raises his cane again over SMIKE]*

NICHOLAS: Wretch! Touch him at your peril. I won't stand by and see it done. By Heaven, I won't spare you, if you drive me on.

SQUEERS: Stand back!

[He strikes at NICHOLAS *with his cane.* NICHOLAS *springs at him, snatches the cane and attacks him with it.* MRS. SQUEERS *shrieks and tries to drag* SQUEERS *away.* NICHOLAS, *having dealt several blows, flings* SQUEERS *from him, and* SQUEERS *and* MRS. SQUEERS *fall in a heap. The* BOYS *raise a feeble cheer, throw paper and pens about and rush from the room towards freedom.* SMIKE *scuttles away to hide in a corner.* SQUEERS *and* MRS. SQUEERS *slowly get up, groaning and rubbing themselves, and silently creep off,* SQUEERS *turning at the door to shake his fist at* NICHOLAS, *who breaks the cane over his knee and flings the pieces after the* SQUEERS. SMIKE *comes from his corner and throws himself at* NICHOLAS's *feet]*

NICHOLAS: Why do you kneel to me, Smike?

SMIKE: Let me go with you, sir. Anywhere, everywhere. To

the world's end. You're my home, my kind friend. Take
me with you.

NICHOLAS: A friend who can do little for you, Smike;
nearly as poor and helpless as yourself.

SMIKE: But may I go with you? I'll be your faithful, hard-
working servant, I will indeed.

NICHOLAS (*raising* SMIKE): And you shall! The world shall
deal by you as it does by me, till one or both of us shall
quit it for a better. Come, Smike.

MISS HAVISHAM'S REVENGE

From *Great Expectations*

Characters:

Charles Dickens

Mrs. Joe

Joe Gargery

Pip

Estella

Miss Havisham

Uncle Pumblechook

DICKENS: Philip Pirrip – no, let us call him Pip, as he is known to his sister and her husband, Mr. and Mrs. Joe Gargery: Pip is an orphan and lives with Mr. and Mrs. Joe in their cottage on the coast of Kent, where Joe is a blacksmith. Today is market day, and Mrs. Joe has just returned from town, bearing with her, in addition to a basket of household goods, something of a more exciting nature. Something, it seems, concerning Pip.

MRS. JOE: Now, if this boy ain't grateful this night, he never will be.

JOE: You mean Pip?

MRS. JOE: What other boy d'you see here?

JOE: Pip, your sister's a master-mind. A master-mind.

PIP: Yes, Joe. What's a master-mind?

JOE: Her.

MRS. JOE. She wants this boy to go and play there.

PIP (*to Joe*): She?

JOE (*to Mrs. Joe*): She?

MRS. JOE: She is a she – unless you call Miss Havisham a he, and I doubt if even you'll go so far as that.

JOE: Miss Havisham up town?

MRS. JOE: Is there any Miss Havisham down town? I tell you, she wants this boy to go and play there. And of course he's going. And he had better play there, or I'll know why.

PIP: Is Miss Havisham the rich old lady who lives in the big house?

JOE: All alone and barricaded against robbers, they say. I wonder how she comes to know Pip?

MRS. JOE: Noodle! Who said she knew him?

JOE: Them who said she wanted him to go and play there.

MRS. JOE: Isn't it just barely possible that Uncle Pumblechook may be a tenant of hers, and that he may sometimes go there to pay his rent? And couldn't she ask Uncle Pumblechook if he knew of a boy to go and play there? And couldn't Uncle Pumblechook, being always considerate and thoughtful for us, then mention this boy that I have for ever been a willing slave to?

JOE: Ah! Now I know.

MRS. JOE: No, Joseph, you may think you know, but you do not. For you don't know yet that Uncle Pumblechook, considering that this boy's fortune may be made by Miss Havisham, has offered to take him with his own hands to Miss Havisham's tomorrow morning. And, Lor-a-mussy-me! here I stand talking to Mooncalfs and the boy grimed with dirt from the hair of his head to the sole of his foot.

PIP (*to audience*): With that, she pounced on me, and I was soaped and kneaded and towelled and thumped until I was quite beside myself, without anyone offering to throw any light on why I was going to play at Miss Havisham's, and what on earth I was expected to play *at*. Mr. Pumblechook and I breakfasted at eight o'clock in the morning and then he took me to Miss Havisham's house, which was of old brick, and dismal, and had a

great many iron bars to it. I was delivered to a young
lady, who was very pretty and very proud, and called
me 'boy' with a carelessness that was far from com-
plimentary. She was about my own age, but seemed
much older than I, and was as scornful of me as if she
had been twenty-one and a queen. The passages in the
house were all dark and she used a candle to light our
way. At last we reached the door of a room.

ESTELLA: Go in.

PIP: After you, miss.

ESTELLA: Don't be ridiculous, boy. I'm not going in.

PIP (*to audience*): She walked away, and, what was worse,
took the candle with her. I was half afraid in the dark,
so I knocked at the door.

MISS HAVISHAM: Enter.

PIP (*to audience*): I found myself in a large, pretty room, well
lighted with candles. No glimpse of daylight was to be
seen. In an armchair sat the strangest lady I have ever
seen. She was dressed in rich materials – satin and lace
and silks – all of white. She had bridal flowers in her
hair – but her hair was white. Some bright jewels
sparkled on her neck and on her hands, and some other
jewels lay sparkling on the table. Dresses and half-packed
trunks were scattered about. Then I saw that everything
which ought to be white was faded and yellow. I saw
that the bride within the bridal dress had withered like
the dress; that the dress had been put upon the rounded
figure of a young woman, and that the figure upon which
it now hung had shrunk to skin and bone. Once, I had
been taken to see a skeleton in the ashes of a rich dress
that had been dug out of a vault under the church pavement. Now, the skeleton seemed to have dark eyes that
moved and looked at me.

MISS HAVISHAM: Who is it?

PIP: Pip, ma'am.

MISS HAVISHAM: Pip?

PIP: The boy Mr. Pumblechook promised to bring, ma'am. Come . . . to play.

MISS HAVISHAM: Come nearer. Let me look at you. Come close. You are not afraid of a woman who has never seen the sun since you were born?

PIP: No, ma'am.

MISS HAVISHAM (*laying her hands on her heart*): Do you know what I touch here?

PIP: Yes, ma'am. Your heart.

MISS HAVISHAM: Broken! I am tired. I want diversion, and I have done with men and women. Play!

PIP: Play, ma'am?

MISS HAVISHAM: I sometimes have sick fancies, and I have a sick fancy that I want to see some play. So, play! Play! Play!

PIP: What at, ma'am?

MISS HAVISHAM: Are you sullen and obstinate?

PIP: No, ma'am. I am very sorry for you, and very sorry I can't play just now. If you complain of me, I shall get into trouble with my sister, so I would play if I could; but it's so new here, and so strange, and . . .

MISS HAVISHAM (*to herself*): So new to him, so old to me. So strange to him, so familiar to me. So melancholy to both of us. (*to* PIP) Call Estella. Surely you can do that? Go to the door and call Estella.

PIP (*calling*): Estella!

MISS HAVISHAM: Is she coming?

PIP: I don't think so.

MISS HAVISHAM: Call again.

PIP: Estella!

MISS HAVISHAM: Is she coming now?

PIP: Yes. I can see her light coming down the passage.

MISS HAVISHAM: Good. Ah, Estella, my dear. Let me see you play cards with this boy.

ESTELLA: With this boy! Why, he is a common labouring boy.

MISS HAVISHAM: Well, you can break his heart.

ESTELLA: What do you play, boy?

PIP: Nothing but beggar my neighbour, miss.

MISS HAVISHAM: Then beggar him!

PIP (*to audience*): Miss Havisham sat, corpse-like, as we played at cards. I began to understand that everything in the room had stopped a long time ago. I knew nothing then of the discoveries that are occasionally made of bodies buried in ancient times, which fall to powder in the moment of being distinctly seen; but I have often thought since that she must have looked as if the natural light of day would have struck her to dust.

ESTELLA: He calls the knaves Jacks, this boy. And what coarse hands he has; and what thick boots. And there, I've won!

MISS HAVISHAM: Are you ready to play again?

PIP (*unhappily*): Yes, ma'am, if I was wanted.

MISS HAVISHAM: Since you are unwilling to play, go into that opposite room, and wait there till I come.

PIP (*to audience*): I crossed the landing and entered the room she indicated. From it, too, the daylight was completely excluded. Candles on the high chimney-piece faintly lighted the chamber, which was spacious, and, I dare say, had once been handsome. But everything in it was covered with dust and mould, and was dropping to pieces. The most prominent object was a long table with a tablecloth spread on it, as if a feast had been in preparation when the house had stopped like a clock. A centrepiece of some kind was in the middle of this cloth. It was so overhung with cobwebs that its form was quite undistinguishable; and I saw speckle-legged spiders with blotchy bodies running home to it and running out from it. I heard the mice, too, rattling behind the panels. Black beetles groped about the hearth.

MISS HAVISHAM (*suddenly*): This is where I shall be laid when I am dead.

PIP (*startled*): Oh!

MISS HAVISHAM: They shall come and look at me here, on this table. What do you think that is? There, where those cobwebs are?

PIP: I . . . I can't guess what it is, ma'am.

MISS HAVISHAM: It's a great cake. A bridal cake. Mine! Do you know, this is my birthday?

PIP: Many happy returns, ma'am.

MISS HAVISHAM: No! I don't allow it to be spoken of. I don't allow anyone to speak of it. On this day of the year, long before you were born, this heap of decay was brought here. It and I have worn away together. The mice have gnawed at it, and sharper teeth than teeth of mice have gnawed at me. When the ruin is complete, and when they lay me dead, in my bride's dress on the bride's table, it will be the finished curse on him – and so much the better if it is done on this day. Estella said many hard things of you, yet you say nothing of her. What do you think of her?

PIP: I don't like to say.

MISS HAVISHAM: Tell me in my ear.

PIP: I think she is very proud.

MISS HAVISHAM: Anything else?

PIP: I think she is very pretty.

MISS HAVISHAM: Anything else?

PIP: I think she is very insulting.

MISS HAVISHAM: Anything else?

PIP: I think I should like to go home.

MISS HAVISHAM: And never see her again, though she is so pretty?

PIP: I am not sure that I shouldn't like to see her again, but I should like to go home now.

MISS HAVISHAM (*calling*): Estella!

ESTELLA: Yes, Miss Havisham?

MISS HAVISHAM: Send him home.

ESTELLA: Very well. (*Whispering to* PIP) Why don't you cry?

PIP: Because I don't want to.

ESTELLA: You do. You are very near crying indeed!

PIP (*to audience*): She laughed, pushed me out, and locked the gate on me. When I reached home my sister was very curious to know all about Miss Havisham's. But I felt that if I described Miss Havisham's as my eyes had seen it, I should not be understood. Not only that, but I felt convinced that Miss Havisham too would not be understood, and it seemed that there would be something coarse and treacherous in my dragging her as she really was before Mrs. Joe and my Uncle Pumblechook, who came at tea time, full of a devouring curiosity.

PUMBLECHOOK: Well, boy, how did you get on up town?

PIP: Pretty well, sir.

PUMBLECHOOK: Pretty well? Pretty well is no answer. Tell us what you mean by pretty well.

PIP: I mean . . . pretty well.

MRS. JOE: Oh, this boy!

PUMBLECHOOK: No, ma'am, pray don't lose your temper. Leave this lad to me. Now, boy, what is Miss Havisham like?

PIP (*lying defiantly*): Very tall and dark.

PUMBLECHOOK: Mm! What was she a-doing of, when you went there today?

PIP: She was . . . sitting in a black velvet coach.

PUMBLECHOOK: ⎫
MRS. JOE: ⎭ In a black velvet coach!

PIP: Yes. And Miss Estella – that's her niece, I think –

handed her in cake and wine at the coach window, on a gold plate. And we all had cake and wine on gold plates. And I got up behind the coach to eat mine, because she told me to.

PUMBLECHOOK: Was anybody else there?

PIP: Four dogs.

PUMBLECHOOK: Large or small?

PIP: Immense. And they fought for veal cutlets out of a silver basket.

MRS. JOE: In the name of gracious, where *was* this coach?

PIP: In Miss Havisham's room.

PUMBLECHOOK: Eh!

PIP: Oh, but there weren't any horses to it.

MRS. JOE: Can this possibly be, Uncle? What can the boy mean?

PUMBLECHOOK: Er, well, I'll tell you, Mum. My opinion is, it's a sedan chair. She's flighty, you know – quite flighty enough to pass her days in a sedan chair. However, the boy went there to play. What did you play at, boy?

PIP: We played with flags.

MRS. JOE: Flags!

PIP: Yes. Estella waved a blue flag, and I waved a red one, and Miss Havisham waved one sprinkled all over with little gold stars, out of the coach window. And then we all waved our swords and hurrahed.

MRS. JOE: Swords! Where did you get swords from?

PIP: Out of a cupboard. And I saw pistols in it – and jam.

PUMBLECHOOK: } Jam!
MRS. JOE:

PIP (*to audience*): If they had asked me any more questions I should undoubtedly have betrayed myself, for I was even then on the point of mentioning that there had been a balloon in the yard. But Mr. Pumblechook drove off soon after, and while my sister was washing up I stole into the forge to Joe and told him all I had said. I remained by him until he had done for the night. Then I said: (*to* JOE) Joe, before the fire goes out, I should like to tell you something.

JOE: Then tell us. What is it, Pip?

PIP: All that about Miss Havisham's . . . It's a terrible thing, Joe. It isn't true.

JOE: Ain't true!

PIP: It's lies, Joe.

JOE: Naw, Pip, not all of it. Why, sure you don't mean to say there was no black velvet coach?

PIP: Yes I do.

JOE: But at least there was dogs, Pip? If there weren't no veal cutlets, at least there was dogs?

PIP: No, Joe.

JOE: *A* dog. A puppy. Come on.

PIP: No, Joe, there was nothing at all of the kind.

JOE: Pip, old chap! This won't do, old fellow. What possessed you?

PIP (*miserably*): I don't know what possessed me, Joe. But I wish you hadn't taught me to call knaves at cards Jacks. And I wish my boots weren't so thick, nor my hands so coarse.

DICKENS: From which we conclude that Miss Havisham, having had her heart broken by the man who jilted her on her wedding day, wants to take her revenge on men; and has chosen Pip, to be made to fall in love with the beautiful Estella, and then, by ridiculing his humble upbringing, to break his heart in turn. To what extent she will succeed is a much longer story.

THE WORST OF TIMES

From *A Tale of Two Cities*

Characters:

Charles Dickens	Jacques Three
Madame Defarge	Miss Pross
Vengeance	Jerry Cruncher

[*N.B. – In the scene between Madame Defarge and Miss Pross, Dickens makes each speak in her own language, neither understanding the other. This would be pointless in this acting version.*]

DICKENS: It was the best of times, it was the worst of times; it was the age of wisdom, it was the age of foolishness; it was the season of Light, it was the season of Darkness; it was the spring of hope, it was the winter of despair. It was, in short, the time of the French Revolution. Charles Darnay, a member of the noble French family of Evremonde, has been sentenced, like many other aristocrats, to be guillotined. His wife, Lucie Darnay, with her small daughter and her father, Dr. Manette, has secretly escaped from her lodging in Paris and is on her way to England. Her companion and servant, Miss Pross and Jerry Cruncher, both of them English, wait their chance to follow; but Madame Defarge, the sinister leader of the Revolutionary women, is seeking personal revenge upon Darnay's family for a wrong done to her sister long before. See her now holding darkly ominous council with two members of the Revolutionary Jury, Jacques Three and a woman named Vengeance.

MADAME DEFARGE: Hear me speak, fellow citizens. My husband is a good Republican.

VENGEANCE: None better in France.

MADAME DEFARGE: And a bold man.

JACQUES: Never a doubt of it.

MADAME DEFARGE: Yet he has his weaknesses. He is so weak as to relent towards these people.

JACQUES: Aye, there's a pity. Something to regret.

VENGEANCE: Not quite like a good citizen.

MADAME DEFARGE: For my part, I care nothing for old Doctor Manette. He may wear his head or lose it, for all I care. But the Evremonde family – they are to be exterminated. The wife and child must follow the husband.

JACQUES: The woman has a fine head for it. I have seen blue eyes and golden hair there before. They looked charming when Samson, the executioner, held them up.

VENGEANCE: The child has golden hair and blue eyes, too. And we seldom have a child there. Such a pretty sight!

MADAME DEFARGE: In a word, then, I cannot trust my husband in this matter. I feel that if I delay there is a danger of his giving warning, and then they might escape.

JACQUES: No one must escape. The guillotine doesn't have half enough as it is. It should have six score a day.

MADAME DEFARGE: I must act for myself, then. She will be at home now, awaiting the moment of his death this afternoon.

VENGEANCE: Three o'clock! I shall be there to see it.

JACQUES: And I!

MADAME DEFARGE: I will go to *her*.

VENGEANCE: Ah, my cherished!

JACQUES: Adorable woman!

MADAME DEFARGE: Take my knitting. Place it in my usual chair before the guillotine to keep it for me. There will be a bigger crowd than ever today.

JACQUES: You will be late?

MADAME DEFARGE: I shall be there before it starts.

VENGEANCE: Before the tumbrils arrive. Be sure to be there before the tumbrils arrive.

MADAME DEFARGE: I would not miss that for the world.

DICKENS: There was no woman at that time more to be dreaded than this ruthless one who now took her way along the streets, a tigress, absolutely without pity. Lying hidden in her bosom was a loaded pistol. It was nothing to her that an innocent man was to die for the sins of his forefathers. It was nothing to her that his wife was to be made a widow and his daughter an orphan. That was insufficient punishment, because they were her natural enemies and her prey.

　　As this fiend drew nearer and nearer to the lodging, Miss Pross and Jerry Cruncher held consultation there about their own departure that afternoon. They would travel in the lightest-wheeled conveyance available to them and would soon catch up the escaping family in the heavier travelling-coach. They would pass it on the road, and so be able to order changes of horses for it in advance.

MISS PROSS: Now, Mr. Cruncher, what do you say to our not starting from this courtyard? One carriage has already gone from here today. Another might awaken suspicion.

JERRY: My opinion, miss, is as you're right.

MISS PROSS: Oh, dear me! I'm so distracted with fear and hope for our precious creatures that I am incapable of forming any plan. Are *you* capable of forming any plan, my dear, good Mr. Cruncher?

JERRY: I think not, miss.

MISS PROSS: If you were to go before and stop the vehicle and horses from coming here, and were to wait somewhere for me – wouldn't that be best?

JERRY: That it might, miss.

MISS PROSS: Now, where could you wait for me? By the cathedral door? Would it be much out of the way to take me into the carriage near the great cathedral door?

JERRY: No, miss.

MISS PROSS: Splendid. Then, like the best of men, go straight to the posting-house and make that change.

JERRY: I don't know about leaving you here alone, miss. We don't know what might happen.

MISS PROSS: Heaven knows we don't. But have no fear for me, Mr. Cruncher. Think only of the lives that may depend on both of us.

JERRY: Miss, I'll stand by you, right or wrong.

MISS PROSS: Dear excellent Mr. Cruncher! Now go.

DICKENS: He immediately went out to alter the arrangements, and left her by herself to follow as she had proposed. Miss Pross got a basin of cold water and began soothing her eyes, which were swollen and red. Haunted by feverish apprehension, she could not bear to have her sight obscured for a minute at a time by the dripping water, but constantly paused and looked round to see that there was no one watching her. In one of those pauses she recoiled and cried out, for she saw a figure standing in the room.

MISS PROSS: Oh!

MADAME DEFARGE: The wife of Evremonde – where is she?

MISS PROSS: My . . . my mistress can see no one.

MADAME DEFARGE: Passing on my way to the guillotine, where they reserve my chair and my knitting for me,

I have called to pay my compliments to her. I wish to see her.

MISS PROSS: I . . . I know your intentions are evil. You may depend on it I'll hold my own against them.

MADAME: Tcha! It will do her no good to keep herself hidden from me. Go tell her I wish to see her, do you hear?

MISS PROSS: You shan't get the better of me. I am an Englishwoman.

MADAME DEFARGE: Pig-like imbecile, I take no answer from you. Either tell her I demand to see her, or stand out of my way and I shall go to her myself.

MISS PROSS: I don't care an English Twopence. I'll not leave a handful of hair on your head if you lay a finger on me.

MADAME DEFARGE: Poor wretch! What are you worth? (*Calling*) Wife of Evremonde! Child of Evremonde! Any person but this miserable fool, answer the Citizeness Defarge! (*Hearing no answer*) What is this? These rooms – they're disordered. There's been hurried packing. There *is* no one in those other rooms! I demand to see.

MISS PROSS: Never.

MADAME DEFARGE: If they are gone they can be pursued and brought back.

MISS PROSS: As long as you don't know whether they are here or are gone you are uncertain what to do. And you shall not know that, if I can prevent it.

MADAME DEFARGE: I will tear you to pieces.

MISS PROSS: We are alone at the top of a high house in a solitary courtyard. We are not likely to be heard. I pray for bodily strength to keep you here. Every minute you are here is worth a hundred thousand guineas to my darling.

[*Madame Defarge grapples with her. After a moment Madame Defarge tries to draw her pistol.*

It goes off in the process and Madame Defarge sinks to the ground]

DICKENS: As the smoke cleared, Miss Pross passed the body as far from it as she could and ran down the stairs, intending to call for fruitless help. She checked herself and went back for the bonnet and other things she must wear. Then she locked the door and took away the key. By good fortune she had a veil on her bonnet, or she could hardly have gone along the streets without being stopped, for the marks of gripping fingers were deep in her face and her hair was torn. In crossing the bridge she dropped the door key in the river. Arriving at the cathedral a few minutes before her escort, and waiting there, she thought, what if the key were already taken in a net, what if it were identified, what if the door were opened and the remains discovered, what if she were stopped, sent to prison and charged with murder! In the midst of these thoughts the carriage arrived and Jerry Cruncher took her in and away.

MISS PROSS: Mr. Cruncher . . .

JERRY: Miss?

MISS PROSS: Isn't there any noise in the streets now?

JERRY: The usual noises, miss.

MISS PROSS: I don't hear you, Mr. Cruncher. What do you say?

JERRY (*a bit louder*): The usual noise, miss. (*to himself*) Cor, bless me, she's gone deaf in an hour. What's come to her?

MISS PROSS: I . . . I feel as if there had been a flash and a crash, and that crash was the last thing I should ever hear in this life.

JERRY: Hark, miss. There's the roll of them dreadful carts. You can't help but hear that, miss. (*A pause*) Cor, she can't!

MISS PROSS: A great crash . . . then a great stillness.

JERRY: If you don't hear the roll of them dreadful carts, it's my opinion that you never *will* hear anything else in this world.

DICKENS: And, indeed, she never did.

AN ADVENTURE IN THE STREETS

From *Dombey & Son*

Characters:

Charles Dickens	Foreman
Florence Dombey	Labourer
Mrs. Brown	Walter Gay

DICKENS: Florence Dombey is the seven-year-old daughter of Paul Dombey, the head of a great London merchant firm. He is not interested in her, but only in his baby son, who will eventually inherit the business; so he leaves her to the care of a nursemaid. One day the nursemaid, Susan, takes Florence on an unauthorized visit to the rough neighbourhood of Camden Town. A bull breaks loose; there is confusion and panic in the crowded street. With a sensation of terror, Florence finds that she is quite alone.

FLORENCE: Susan! Susan! Oh, where is she? Where is she?

MRS. BROWN (*very oily*): Where's who, dearie?

FLORENCE (*startled*): Oh! Oh, my ... Susan, my nurse.

MRS. BROWN: Why did you run away from her?

FLORENCE: I was frightened. I didn't know what I did. I ... I thought she was with me.

MRS. BROWN: Well, you just come along o' me, dearie, and I'll show you where she is.

FLORENCE: Oh!

MRS. BROWN: You needn't be frightened now. (*Harsher*) Come along!

FLORENCE (*frightened*): I ... I don't know you.

MRS. BROWN: I'm Mrs. Brown. *Good* Mrs. Brown.

FLORENCE: All right, then. Is Susan near here?

MRS. BROWN: Oh, aye. Susan an't far off.

FLORENCE: Did anybody get hurt?

MRS. BROWN: Not a bit of it.

DICKENS: The child accompanied the old woman willingly; though she could not help glancing at her face as they went along and wondering whether *Bad* Mrs. Brown, if there were such a person, was like her at all. They had not gone far when the old woman turned down a dirty lane and stopped before a shabby little house. Opening the door with a key she took out of her bonnet, she pushed the child before her into a back room, where there was a great heap of rags of different colours lying on the floor. There was no furniture at all, and the walls and ceiling were quite black.

FLORENCE: Why have you brought me here? I don't like this place.

MRS. BROWN: Now don't be a young mule. I'm not going to hurt you. Sit on them rags.

FLORENCE: But ...

MRS. BROWN: Sit, I tell you!

FLORENCE: Very well.

MRS. BROWN: I'm not a-goin' to keep you above an hour. D'ye understand?

FLORENCE: Yes.

MRS. BROWN: Then don't vex me. If you don't, I tell you I won't hurt you. But if you do, I'll kill you.

FLORENCE: Oh, oh!

MRS. BROWN: Oh, yes. I could have killed you at any time – even if you was in your own bed at home. Now, let's know who you are, and what you are, and all about it.

FLORENCE: I ... I'm called Florence Dombey.

MRS. BROWN: Dombey, eh? Not Dombey & Son?

FLORENCE: Yes.

MRS. BROWN: Well, well, well. In that case, I want that pretty frock o' yours, *Miss* Dombey. And that little bonnet, and a petticoat or two, and anything else you can spare.

FLORENCE: No!

MRS. BROWN: Yes! Come, take 'em off. (*Very menacing*) D'ye hear me?

FLORENCE: Why do you want them?

MRS. BROWN: To sell, of course. Gotter keep body and soul together, an't I? Good. And I'll take the shoes, too. Yes, I must have the shoes.

FLORENCE (*a little cry of pain*): Ow!

MRS. BROWN: What's the matter? I an't touched you – yet.

FLORENCE: It's my bonnet. It caught in my hair.

MRS. BROWN: Your hair? Oh, lor', why couldn't you ha' let me be?

FLORENCE (*thoroughly frightened*): What do you mean? I don't know what I've done.

MRS. BROWN: Just when I was contented.

FLORENCE: What are you going to do with those scissors? No! Don't come near!

MRS. BROWN: I can't help it, don't you see? I want them curls o' yours.

FLORENCE: No! Please!

MRS. BROWN: Anybody but me would have had 'em off first of all. Fetches a good price, does nice long hair. There! Lovely! Now another ... Oh, if I hadn't once had a gal of my own that was proud of her hair I'd have had every lock of it. (*Beginning to sob*) But she's beyond the seas now. Far away. Oh, far away!

FLORENCE: Please – you're hurting.

MRS. BROWN: Ah, well, that'll do, I dare say. Now, then, move aside off them rags and let's see what Good Mrs.

Brown can give you in fair exchange. See – here's a pretty dress.

FLORENCE: It's all torn.

MRS. BROWN: Never you mind that. Just put it on.

FLORENCE: No!

MRS. BROWN: You'll do as I say, *Miss* Dombey. Good. Oh, look at this dear cloak.

FLORENCE: It's filthy! Oh – there are things crawling on it!

MRS. BROWN: And this bonnet. Fit for any lady.

FLORENCE: Ugh!

MRS. BROWN: You get 'em all on, and quick about it. And then . . .

FLORENCE (*very alarmed*): W-what?

MRS. BROWN (*a cackle of laughter*): That made you wonder, didn't it? Well, all I'm a-goin' to do is lead you to some street where you can start findin' yer own way.

FLORENCE: Oh, thank you.

MRS. BROWN: But mind, you're goin' to do it just as I say.

FLORENCE: I promise I will.

MRS. BROWN: Good. You'll stand just where I leave you till the clocks strike three. Then you can set off for your Pa's place in the City. But, mind, don't you tell no one about me, or start looking for this place again. D'ye understand?

FLORENCE: Yes.

MRS. BROWN: Because, remember, there'll be eyes and ears to tell me if you disobey, and I could come and kill you any time I choose. Any time at all.

DICKENS: At length Mrs. Brown conducted her changed and ragged little friend through a labyrinth of narrow streets and alleys. Reminding her to stand still until the clocks struck three, she left her. Still sorely afraid, Florence remained there, looking at the bustle in the street. The clocks appeared to have made up their minds never to strike three any more, but at last one rang out, and Florence hurried off as fast as she could. All she knew of her father's offices was that they were in the City. But by asking her way to the City she advanced by slow degrees, stunned by the noise and confusion, terrified by what she had undergone and the prospect of encountering her angry father. It was full two hours later in the afternoon when she peeped into a kind of wharf on the riverside and saw a stout man standing there, with his pen behind his ear.

FLORENCE: Please, sir . . .

FOREMAN: Now, then! We haven't anything for beggars here. Be off!

FLORENCE: If you please, is this the City?

FOREMAN: Aye, it's the City. You know that well enough, I dare say. Now be off!

FLORENCE: I don't want anything, thank you, except to know the way to Dombey & Son's.

FOREMAN: Eh! What can the likes of you want with Dombey & Son's?

FLORENCE: To know the way there, if you please.

FOREMAN: Here, half a minute. (*Calling*) Joe!

JOE: 'allo?

FOREMAN: Where's that young clerk o' Dombey's who's been watching them goods shipped?

JOE: Young Walter Gay? He's here. Just goin'.

FOREMAN: Then send him here a minute.

JOE: Right!

WALTER: Do you want me, Mr. Clark?

FOREMAN: Look'ye here.

WALTER: Who . . .?

FLORENCE: Please, I'm lost. I was lost this morning, a long way from here – and I've had my clothes taken away and had to put these on. And my name's Florence Dombey . . .

WALTER: Florence Dombey!

FLORENCE (*beginning to cry*): Yes.

WALTER: Miss Florence, please don't cry. You are as safe now as if you were guarded by a whole boat's crew from a man-o'-war. Give me your arm and I will take you to your father at once. And just let me see the villain who will dare molest you now.

FOREMAN: Well, I never saw the like on this wharf before!

DICKENS: And nor, we dare say, did he again. So Florence's adventure ended. Little did she know at the time, but it had been a double adventure for her. It had brought her together with young Walter Gay, who one day would be her husband and the means of reconciling her with her cold, proud father.

SCHOOL FOR THIEVES

From *Oliver Twist*

DICKENS: Once upon a time it was thought coarse and shocking that some of the characters in this novel are chosen from the most criminal and degraded of London's population. But it appeared to me that to draw a knot of such associates in crime as really did exist; to show them as they really were, for ever skulking uneasily through the dirtiest paths of life, with the great black ghastly gallows closing up their prospect; it appeared to me that to do this would be to attempt something which was needed, and which would be a service to society. Oliver Twist, an orphan, brought up in a workhouse, sent out to earn his living at the age of nine, and bullied by his master's apprentice, runs away towards London and, after a week of tramping, finds himself in the little town of Barnet, where he sinks down on a doorstep in the busy main street.

[*While he has been speaking these last lines,* OLIVER *has entered wearily, to sink down as described. He buries his face in his hands and sobs quietly.* JACK DAWKINS *strolls up and stands looking at him*]

DAWKINS: Hullo, my covey! What's the row?

OLIVER: I ... I am very hungry and tired. I have walked a long way. I have been walking these seven days.

DAWKINS (*whistles*): Walkin' for sivin days! Oh, I see. Beak's order, eh? Only I don't suppose you know what a beak is, eh?

OLIVER: No.

DAWKINS: My eyes, how green! A beak's a magistrate. You goin' to London?

OLIVER: Yes.

DAWKINS: Got any lodgings?

OLIVER: No.

DAWKINS: Money?

OLIVER: No. Do you live in London?

DAWKINS: I do when I'm at home. I suppose you want some place to sleep tonight, don't you?

OLIVER: I do indeed. I haven't slept under a roof since I left the country.

DAWKINS: Well, don't fret your eyelids on that score. I've got to be in London tonight, and I know a 'spectable old gen'lman as lives there wot'll give you lodgings for nothink, and never ask for the change. That is, if any gen'lman he knows introduces you.

OLIVER: Does he know you?

DAWKINS: Don't he? Oh, no! Not in the least! By no means! Certainly not! Come on, young shaver, and you'll see if Jack Dawkins and 'is friend is welcome or not. I'm at low water-mark myself – only a bob in my pocket – but you want some grub first, and you shall have it.

DICKENS: Assisting Oliver to rise, the young gentleman took

him to an adjacent shop, where he purchased ham and a loaf. Oliver made a hearty meal, after which they set forth together on the road to London. The Artful Dodger, as Jack Dawkins explained he was known to his intimate friends, led the way at a rapid pace through Islington into Saffron Hill. A dirtier or more wretched place Oliver had never seen. The street was very narrow and muddy, children screamed everywhere and drunken men and women positively wallowed in filth. Oliver was just considering whether he hadn't better run away when the Dodger caught him by the arm, pushed open the door of a house and drew him quickly inside. The walls and ceiling of the room were black with age and dirt. In front of the fire was a very old, shrivelled man, with a villainous-looking face and dressed in a greasy flannel gown. Four boys, smoking long clay pipes and drinking spirits with the air of middle-aged men, were sorting a great number of silk handkerchiefs at a table.

DAWKINS: Hullo, Fagin.

FAGIN: Dodger, my dear! But there's two of you.

DAWKINS: This here's my friend, Oliver Twist.

FAGIN (*bowing low*): Oliver, eh? We're very glad to see you, Oliver, very. One of you take Oliver's cap and hang it up for him. Somebody give him a chair near the fire. And keep them hands out of his pockets, or I'll lay this toasting-fork across you! Ah, Oliver, my dear, you're a-starin' at the handkerchiefs, I see. There are a good many of 'em, ain't there? We've just looked 'em out ready for the wash, eh, lads?

[*All except* OLIVER *laugh heartily*]

Charley Bates here *made* all these – didn't you, Charley?

[*Laughter again*]

He's a good boy, ain't you, Charley? Very well *made*. Only you ain't marked some of 'em too well. The marks will have to be picked out again with a needle.

[*More laughter*]

Perhaps we'll teach Oliver how to do it, eh? Shall us, Oliver?

OLIVER: If you please, sir.

FAGIN: You'd like to be able to make pocket handkerchiefs as easy as Charley, wouldn't you, my dear?

OLIVER: Very much indeed, if you'll teach me, sir.

[*Loud laughter from the rest*]

FAGIN: Now, Dodger, I hope you've been working hard today?

DAWKINS: Hard as nails, Fagin.

FAGIN: Good boy, good boy. What have you made?

DAWKINS: A couple of wallets.

FAGIN: Well *lined*, I hope?

DAWKINS: Pretty well. Here they are.

FAGIN: Hm! Not quite so heavy as they might be. But very neat and nicely made. Ingenious workman, ain't he, Oliver?

OLIVER: Very indeed, sir.

[*Laughter*]

FAGIN: Well, all work and no play ... It's time for our game, boys. Dodger and Charley first.

OTHERS: Yes!

FAGIN: You sit and watch, Oliver, and then you can learn to play.

[*Act out the following speech*]

DICKENS: Placing a snuff-box in one pocket of his trousers, a wallet in another, and a watch in his waistcoat pocket, and sticking a diamond pin in his shirt, Fagin buttoned his coat tight round him. Having put his spectacle-case and handkerchief in his coat pockets, he took a stick and trotted up and down the room in imitation of the manner in which old gentlemen walk about the streets. Sometimes he stopped at the fireplace, and sometimes at the door, making believe that he was staring with all his might into shop windows. At such times he would look constantly round him, for fear of thieves, and would keep slapping all his pockets in turn, to see that he hadn't lost anything, in such a very funny and natural manner that Oliver laughed till the tears ran down his face. All this time the Dodger and Charley followed him closely about, getting out of his sight nimbly every time he turned round. At last the Dodger trod upon his toes, as though accidentally, while Charley Bates stumbled up against him behind; and in that one moment they took from him, with the most extraordinary rapidity, snuff-box, wallet, watch, diamond pin, and spectacle-case. But as Charley was removing the handkerchief, Fagin cried out and seized his wrist, and then the things had to be put back and the game begun all over again with two of the other boys.

FAGIN (*to* OLIVER): There, my dear, that's a pleasant game, isn't it?

OLIVER: Oh, very good, sir.

> [*Laughter*]

FAGIN: Is my handkerchief hanging out of my pocket, my dear?

OLIVER: Yes, sir.

FAGIN: Then see if you can take it out without my feeling it, as you saw them do.

> [OLIVER *gingerly takes the handkerchief*, FAGIN *winking at the other boys unseen by him*]

Is it gone yet?

OLIVER: Yes, sir. Here it is.

FAGIN: My word, what a clever boy! I never saw a sharper boy. Here's a shilling for you, my dear.

OLIVER: Thank you, sir!

FAGIN: If you go in this way you'll be the greatest man of the time. And now, the rest of you, be off!

OTHERS: Right, Fagin.

[*They go*]

FAGIN: There, my dear. They've gone for the rest of the day.

OLIVER: Have they gone back to work, sir?

FAGIN: Yes. That is, unless they should unexpectedly come across any while they're out, and then they won't neglect it if they do. Make 'em your models, my dear. Make 'em your models, do everything they bid you, and take their advice in all matters – especially the Dodger's, my dear. He'll be a great man himself and will make you one too, if you take your pattern from him. But now, my dear, you'd like something to eat and drink, I can see, and then a nice sleep, after which old Fagin will teach you how to take the marks out of handkerchiefs with a needle.

DICKENS: It was late when Oliver awoke from a sound, long sleep. There was no other person in the room but Fagin. He was stooping, and as Oliver watched drowsily he drew forth, as it seemed from some trap in the floor, a small box, which he placed carefully on the table. Dragging a chair up to the table, he sat down and took from the box a magnificent gold watch, sparkling with jewels.

FAGIN: Aha! Clever dogs! Staunch to the last! Went to the gallows without telling where the jewels were. Never peached upon old Fagin! And why should they? It wouldn't have loosened the knot, or kept the drop up a minute longer. Fine fellows! Fine fellows!

DICKENS: He once more deposited the watch in its place of safety. At least half a dozen more were then drawn forth from the box and surveyed with equal pleasure, besides rings, brooches, bracelets and other articles of magnificent jewellery.

FAGIN: What a fine thing capital punishment is! Dead men never repent. Dead men never bring awkward stories to light. Ah, it's a fine thing for the trade! Five of 'em strung up in a row, and none left to turn white-livered.

DICKENS: As Fagin uttered these words his bright dark eyes, which had been staring vacantly before him, fell on Oliver's face. He closed the lid of the box with a loud crash; and, laying his hand on a bread knife which was on the table, started furiously up.

FAGIN: What's that? What do you watch me for? Why are you awake? Speak out, boy. What have you seen?

OLIVER: I wasn't able to sleep any longer, sir. I am very sorry I have disturbed you, sir.

FAGIN: Were you awake an hour ago?

OLIVER: No, sir.

FAGIN (*very threatening*): Are you sure?

OLIVER: On my word, sir.

DICKENS: Fagin raised the knife, as if to strike. He trembled very much. Even in his terror, Oliver could see that the knife quivered in the air. Then the old man abruptly resumed his former manner, playing with the knife a little before he laid it down, as if to induce the belief that he had been caught up in mere sport.

FAGIN: Of course I knew that, my dear. I only tried to frighten you. You're a brave boy, Oliver.

OLIVER: Thank you, sir.

FAGIN: Did you see any of those pretty things, my dear?

OLIVER: Yes, sir.

FAGIN: Ah! They ... they're mine, Oliver. My little property. All I have to live upon in my old age. The folks call me a miser, my dear. Only a miser, that's all.

DICKENS: Oliver thought the old gentleman must be a decided miser to live in such a dirty place, with so many watches; but, thinking that perhaps his fondness for the Dodger and the other boys cost him a good deal of money, he only cast a deferential look at Fagin and asked if he might get up. For many days Oliver remained in that room, picking the marks out of pocket-handker-chiefs and sometimes taking part in the game already described. At length Fagin told him he might go out under the joint guardianship of Charley Bates and the Artful Dodger.

[*The scene is acted out*]

The three boys sallied out, the Dodger with his coat-sleeves turned up and his hat cocked as usual; Master Bates sauntering along with his hands in his pockets; and Oliver between them, wondering where they were going, and what branch of manufacture he would be instructed in first. They were just emerging from a narrow court in Clerkenwell when they saw a very respectable-looking old gentleman who had taken up a book from a stall and was standing reading away as hard as if he were in his own study. The Dodger made a sudden stop, laying his finger on his lip.

OLIVER: What's the matter?

DAWKINS: Ssh! See that old cove at the book stall?

OLIVER: The old gentleman? Yes, I see him.

DAWKINS: He'll do.

BATES: A prime plant!

DICKENS: The two boys walked stealthily across the road and slunk close behind the old gentleman. Oliver walked a few paces after them, and stood looking on in silent amazement. What was his horror and alarm to see the Dodger plunge his hand into the old gentleman's pocket and draw out his handkerchief. He handed it to Charley Bates and both ran away round the corner at full speed.

OLD GENTLEMAN (*turning round without seeing the running boys*): Stop thief!

PASSERS-BY (*rushing on*): Stop thief! Stop thief!

DICKENS: In an instant the whole mystery of the hand-kerchiefs, and the watches, and the jewels rushed through the boy's mind. He stood for a moment with the blood tingling through all his veins from terror. Then, confused and not knowing what he did, he took to his heels.

OLD GENTLEMAN: Stop thief!

PASSERS-BY: Stop thief!

DICKENS: In an instant he was brought down upon the pavement by a hard blow, the crowd eagerly gathering round him, jostling with one another to catch a glimpse.

FIRST MAN: Give him air!

SECOND MAN: He don't deserve any.

THIRD MAN: Make way! Make way for the gent! Here he is, sir.

OLD GENTLEMAN: I am afraid he's hurt.

SECOND MAN: I did that, sir. Cut my knuckles on his mouth, I did. Come on, you. Get up!

OLIVER: It wasn't me, sir. Sir, it was two other boys.

PASSERS-BY (*laugh and jeer*).

OLIVER: They're here somewhere.

POLICEMAN (*coming up*): Oh no they ain't. You come with me.

OLIVER: No, please!

OLD GENTLEMAN: Don't hurt him, officer.

POLICEMAN: Oh no, I won't hurt him! Come on!

> [*The crowd gives a final great cheer and jeer as Oliver is roughly marched away, leaving the old gentleman sadly shaking his head as he watches them go*]

DICKENS: Thus, in the very moment when Oliver realized that his new associates were thieves, he found himself branded as one of them and dragged before a magistrate. How he escaped the clutch of the law and of the villainous Fagin, and how he was recaptured by the latter and made to take part in a robbery, belong to the full story of the Life and Adventures of Oliver Twist.

BARDELL *v.* PICKWICK

The saga of Bardell versus Pickwick, from *The Pickwick Papers*, is one of the funniest episodes in all literature. At the age of only twenty-four Dickens took wings when he wrote it and soared from obscurity to immediate fame. The story is ingenious and often hilarious; the characters include several immortals – Sam and Tony Weller, Serjeant Buzfuz, Mrs. Bardell, Snodgrass, Tupman, Winkle, and, of course, Samuel Pickwick himself; and the 'send-up' of the law and its processes is trenchant.

The breach of promise suit and its consequences is, of course, only one of the many ingredients of *The Pickwick Papers*, which appeared in monthly parts during 1836–7, where it is interspersed with other episodes. What we have done is to draw together the chief elements of the story into a compact dramatization which (we hope) serves the threefold purpose of telling the rounded story, accommodating all the great characters in typical vein, and presenting most of those episodes which are minutely familiar to, and ever-loved by, Dickens enthusiasts throughout the world.

So, as a play, it has several 'star' roles to offer. Perhaps Sam Weller, as Narrator and as himself, deserves top billing, with Pickwick just below. But, undoubtedly, the most formidable challenge must be faced by the actor who plays Serjeant Buzfuz. With his long speeches, replete with irony and mock emotion, he must dominate the great trial scene which is the heart of the play. Yet, even in such relatively small-part characterizations as the Judge, Mrs. Cluppins, Solomon Pell and Nathaniel Winkle there is scope for little gems of performance, while the part of Tony Weller is a gift for the right actor.

The story is presented here as a continuous piece of action, punctuated by the narration of Sam Weller, who steps out of and back into the action for the purpose. This means that, as in Shakespeare's method, scenery is quite unnecessary and there is no need to break the flow by lowering the curtain or extinguishing the lights. Strictly speaking, no properties are needed, either; though to avoid having all the characters standing up all the time it is desirable that a few chairs should be on stage, where they can be moved as necessary by the actors themselves. The trial scene will require the Judge to occupy some form of dais and the other occupants of the court to be seated as we have indicated in the text. The play can be acted in the classroom or on an open stage with only drapes for background; or, as producers will recognize, there is ample scope for full-scale presentation, with each scene fully dressed or at least sketched by means of flown backdrops and a judicious choice of furnishings and properties.

We should like, in offering this play, to acknowledge the inspiration which brought it into being. We first wrote *Bardell* v. *Pickwick* as a ninety-minute 'Saturday-Night Theatre' play for Radio 4 of the British Broadcasting Corporation, which presented it with great success near to Christmas 1968. This suggested to us at once that a shortened version for stage could make a play for schools and amateurs that would provide important parts for several actors and plenty of enjoyment for their supporting cast, not to mention, we trust, for their audiences.

BARDELL *v.* PICKWICK

From *The Pickwick Papers*

The action as presented here is continuous, but, divided into Scenes, the sequence runs as follows:

Characters:

SAM WELLER: Pickwick's valet. A fresh young Cockney.

SAMUEL PICKWICK: Portly, bald, beaming, bespectacled and benevolent.

MRS. BARDELL: Pickwick's landlady. A comely widow.

TOMMY BARDELL: Her small son. A bit of a horror.

TRACY TUPMAN: A member of the Pickwick Club. Well-fed and rather pompous.

AUGUSTUS SNODGRASS: A member of the Pickwick Club. Lean and poetic-looking.

NATHANIEL WINKLE: A member of the Pickwick Club. Rather dashing, but with a nervous stutter.

DODSON: A solicitor. Plump, loud-voiced and over-bearing.

FOGG: Dodson's partner.

JACKSON: Their clerk. (He is heard but not seen.)

TONY WELLER: Sam's father. A fat, beery coachman.

PERKER: Pickwick's solicitor. A dry little man.

THE JUDGE: Vague and irritable.

SERJEANT BUZFUZ: Red-faced, domineering and full of tricks.

SERJEANT SNUBBIN: Lean and dusty.

MRS. CLUPPINS: Mrs. Bardell's friend. Thin and shrill.

FOREMAN OF THE JURY

JURYMEN

SPECTATORS IN COURT

LAWYERS AND COURT OFFICIALS

SOLOMON PELL: An attorney. Fat, pale and very Jewish.

COBBLER: An old, emaciated, dying man.

TWO PRISONERS

[*N.B.* – 'Serjeant' was the title borne by the highest class of barristers until 1880. *Bardell* v. *Pickwick* is set in 1830.]

> [SAM WELLER *enters and comes down to address the audience*]

SAM: Evenin', one and all. Sam Veller's the monicker, late of the White Hart Inn, High Street, Borough, and wery glad indeed to be out of it, as the turkey said arter he flew out of the oven. It was done on account of a hamiable old party, Mr. Samuel Pickvick, Esquire, who must of took a fancy to yours truly ven staying at the White Hart vith his three young friends, Messrs. Tupman,

Snodgrass and Winkle, who called themselves the Pickvick Club. He sent for me one morning to his rooms in
Goswell Street by a young shaver, name of Bardell. And
what I vosn't to know till later vos that while we was makin'
our way to the old gent's place, he vos gettin' hisself
into a rare old tangle vith *Mrs.* Bardell, 'is landlady.
(*Winking, as he exits into the wings*) Oh, a rare old tangle!

> [PICKWICK'S *lodging.* PICKWICK *stands with
> his back to the audience, hands clasped behind his
> back, looking down from the window into the street.*
> MRS. BARDELL *is flicking about with a feather
> duster behind him.* PICKWICK *turns round and
> consults his watch*]

PICKWICK: Hm! Your little boy is a very long time gone,
Mrs. Bardell.

MRS. BARDELL: Why, it's a good long way to the Borough,
sir.

PICKWICK: Hm! Yes, yes. So it is. (*He looks at her keenly,
then clears his throat*) Er, Mrs. Bardell ...

MRS. BARDELL (*still dusting*): Sir?

PICKWICK: Do you, ah, think it a much greater expense to
keep two people, than to keep one?

> [MRS. BARDELL *freezes into suspended animation,
> the duster poised. She straightens up slowly*]

MRS. BARDELL: La, Mr. Pickwick! What a question to put
to a widow!

PICKWICK: Well, but *do* you?

MRS. BARDELL (*becoming coy*): That depends ... it depends
a good deal upon the person; and whether it's a saving
and careful person.

PICKWICK: Very true. But the person I have in my eye,
Mrs. Bardell, I think possesses all these qualities.

MRS. BARDELL (*blushing furiously*): La, Mr. Pickwick!

PICKWICK: To tell the truth, Mrs. Bardell, I have made
up my mind. You'll think it very strange, now, that I

never consulted you about this matter, and never ever
mentioned it till I sent your boy out this morning.

MRS. BARDELL: So ... then you sent him to the Borough
on some errand, sir, so as to ... Oh, you're very kind to
a poor widow, sir.

PICKWICK: The arrangement will save you a good deal of
trouble, at least.

MRS. BARDELL: Oh, I never thought anything of the
trouble, sir. And of course I should take more trouble
to please you then than ever. But it is so kind of you,
Mr. Pickwick, to have so much consideration for my
loneliness.

PICKWICK (*surprised*): Your ... Ah, to be sure. I never
thought of that. You'll always have someone to sit with
you. Exactly!

MRS. BARDELL (*dabbing her eyes*): I'm sure I ought to be a
very happy woman.

PICKWICK: And your little boy – Tommy.

MRS. BARDELL (*loud sob*): Bless his heart!

PICKWICK: He, too, will have a companion – a lively one,
who will teach him, I'll be bound, more tricks in a week
than he would ever learn in a year.

MRS. BARDELL: Oh, you dear!

PICKWICK: Eh?

MRS. BARDELL: You kind, good, playful dear! I'll never
leave you – dear, good kind soul!

> [*With a long, rapturous sigh she faints into* PICK-
> WICK'S *arms. He stands there holding her, be-
> wildered*]

PICKWICK: Bless my soul! Mrs. Bardell, my good creature,
pray compose yourself. Let go of me. I hear someone
coming up the stairs. Gracious heavens!

> [*The door flies open and* TUPMAN, SNODGRASS
> *and* WINKLE *enter in a rush, to pull up short and
> stare amazedly*]

TUPMAN
NODGRASS } (*together*): Pickwick!
WINKLE

> [TOMMY BARDELL *rushes in past them and begins to pummel* PICKWICK *furiously*]

TOMMY: Me ma! What you doin' to me ma, you old ...!

PICKWICK: Tupman! Snodgrass! Winkle! Get this young villain off me, do you hear?

> [*They pull* TOMMY *away, his fists still flailing.* TUPMAN *holds him still*]

Thank you. Now help me with this woman.

> [WINKLE *and* SNODGRASS *take the weight of* MRS. BARDELL, *who slumps between them*]

MRS. BARDELL (*a groan*).

TOMMY (*nearly escaping*): Ma!

TUPMAN: Silence, boy!

WINKLE: Pickwick, w-what on earth has been ha-happening?

PICKWICK: She fainted into my arms.

> [*His three friends exchange glances with one another*]

I cannot conceive what can be the matter with her. I had merely announced to her my intention of keeping a manservant. She fell into a most extraordinary paroxysm, flung herself upon me, and ... and fainted. Most extraordinary.

> [TUPMAN *clears his throat and looks at the others*]

TUPMAN: Very.

PICKWICK: Placed me in such an extremely awkward situation.

SNODGRASS: *Very.*

MRS. BARDELL (*groans*).

SNODGRASS: She's coming to. Winkle, help me lead her downstairs. Can you walk, madam?

MRS. BARDELL (*weakly*): Thank you, sir – thank you.

SNODGRASS: Then pray come along. That's right.

[SNODGRASS *and* WINKLE *bear the sagging*
MRS. BARDELL *through the door.* TOMMY *makes*
to run after them, but TUPMAN *holds him*
firmly]

PICKWICK: Tupman, you're surely not thinking . . .

TUPMAN: A manservant, did you say, Pickwick? Well,
there's a person in the passage. I believe this boy brought
him.

PICKWICK: Precisely. Tupman, please have the goodness
to send him in.

TUPMAN: Very well. Now, come along, my boy, and you
shall see your mother directly.

[TUPMAN *escorts* TOMMY *off*]

PICKWICK: Dear me, dear me! Extraordinary behaviour
for a woman. I shall have to engage new lodgings at
once.

[SAM WELLER *enters jauntily*]

Ah, there you are, my good man.

SAM: Here I am, sir. Sam Veller at your service.

PICKWICK: You remember me? I encountered you at the
White Hart Inn.

SAM: Never to be forgotten, sir, as the man said when the
elephant trod on him.

PICKWICK: I want to speak to you. I wish to know whether
you have any reason to be discontented with your
present situation. Boots, isn't it?

SAM: Afore I answers that 'ere question, sir, I should like to
know whether you're going to provide me with a better
one?

PICKWICK: I *have* half made up my mind to engage you.

SAM: Wages?

PICKWICK: Twelve pounds a year.

SAM: Clothes?

PICKWICK: Two suits.

SAM: Work?

PICKWICK: To attend on me and travel about with me and my three friends of the Pickwick Club as we pursue our aim of enlarging our sphere of observation, thus advancing our knowledge.

SAM: Take the bill down, then. I'm let to a single gen'lman and the terms is agreed upon.

PICKWICK: Splendid!

> [PICKWICK *wrings* SAM's *hand and exits.* SAM *comes down to the audience*]

SAM: Vell, vot with travelling about, running errands, showin' folks in, and what all, I soon didn't know vether I wos meant to be footman, groom, gamekeeper or seedsman. I looks like a compo of every one on 'em.

> [*He produces a long envelope and flourishes it*]

And a postman.

> [PICKWICK *bustles in, followed by* TUPMAN, SNODGRASS *and* WINKLE, *and catches sight of the envelope*]

PICKWICK: Ah, Sam. What have you there?

SAM: Called at the Post Office just now, sir, and found this here letter for you.

> [PICKWICK *takes the envelope and examines it*]

PICKWICK: I don't know this hand.

WINKLE: W-why not open it?

PICKWICK: *Thank* you, Winkle.

> [*He rips open the envelope and draws out a letter, which he unfolds and begins to read. His expression becomes one of horror and he staggers back, to be caught by* TUPMAN *and* SNODGRASS]

Mercy on us, what's this?

TUPMAN (*peering over* PICKWICK's *shoulder at the letter*): What is it?

PICKWICK: It must be a jest!

SNODGRASS: Ah!

PICKWICK: It can't be true!

WINKLE: Nobody d-dead, what?

> [PICKWICK *hands the letter to* TUPMAN, *fishe*
> *out his handkerchief and begins mopping his brow*]

PICKWICK: Tupman, please – I can't.

TUPMAN: Certainly. (*He unfolds the letter and reads it out*
'Freeman's Court, Cornhill, August 28th, 1830. Bardel
against Pickwick.'

SNODGRASS: }
WINKLE: } What?

TUPMAN: 'Bardell against Pickwick. Sir, having been in
structed by Mrs. Martha Bardell to commence ar
action against you for breach of promise of marriage . . .

SNODGRASS: }
WINKLE: } Breach of promise!

TUPMAN (*frowning at them*): '. . . breach of promise o
marriage, for which the plaintiff lays her damages a
fifteen hundred pounds . . .'

WINKLE: F-f-fif . . .

> [*He catches* TUPMAN'S *eye and falls silent*]

TUPMAN: '. . . we beg to inform you that a writ has beer
issued against you in this suit in the Court of Commor
Pleas, and request to know, by return of post, the name
of your attorney in London who will accept service
thereof. We are, sir, your obedient servants, Dodson and
Fogg.'

WINKLE (*mechanically*): D-Dodson and Fogg.

SNODGRASS: Bardell against Pickwick.

PICKWICK: It's a conspiracy! A base conspiracy between
these two grasping attorneys. They have persuaded her
to act in order to gain a fee for themselves.

WINKLE: Sh-shame!

PICKWICK: Mrs. Bardell would never do it. She hasn't the
heart to. She hasn't the *case* to do it. Ridiculous!

TUPMAN: Of her heart, Pickwick, you should certainly be
the best judge. I don't wish to discourage you, but I

should certainly say that, of her case, Dodson and Fogg are far better judges than any of us can be.

PICKWICK: Rubbish! A vile attempt to extort money. Why, whoever heard me address her in any way but that in which a lodger would address his landlady?

[*The others look uncomfortable*]

Whoever saw me with her? Not even you, my friends ...

WINKLE: Except on w-one occasion – eh?

PICKWICK: What, Winkle? Explain yourself, sir.

WINKLE: Well, I m-mean, she was certainly reclining in your arms.

PICKWICK: She ... (*thunderstruck*) Gracious powers!

SNODGRASS: And you were soothing her anguish, poor woman.

PICKWICK: I don't deny it, Snodgrass. But she fainted. She ... Oh, what a dreadful instance of the force of circumstances! I'll have it explained, though. I'll see this Dodson and Fogg. I'll see them myself, tomorrow.

[*He exits slowly, shaking his head.* TUPMAN, SNODGRASS *and* WINKLE *follow.* SAM *comes down to the audience*]

SAM (*winking*): Rum feller, the hemperor. Think of his making up to that Mrs. Bardell. And her vith a little boy, too! Always the vay vith these here old 'uns, as is such steady goers to look at.

[*He winks broadly and walks back into the action in* DODSON & FOGG'S *office as the two partners enter with* PICKWICK]

FOGG: And here is my partner, Mr. Dodson. This is Mr. Pickwick, Dodson.

DODSON: Ah! You are the defendant, sir, in Bardell against Pickwick?

PICKWICK: I am, sir. And this is my manservant, Sam Weller.

DODSON: Really? And now, sir, what do you propose?

FOGG: Yes, Mr. Pickwick. What *do* you propose?

DODSON: Hush, Fogg. Let me hear what Mr. Pickwick has to say.

PICKWICK: I came, gentlemen, to express the surprise with which I received your letter and to enquire what grounds of action you can have against me.

FOGG: Grounds of . . .!

DODSON: Mr. Fogg, *I* am going to speak.

FOGG: I beg your pardon, Mr. Dodson.

DODSON: I do not hesitate to say, sir, that our grounds of action, sir, are strong and not to be shaken. You may be an unfortunate man, sir, or you may be a designing one; but if I were called upon, as a juryman upon my oath, sir, to express an opinion of your conduct, sir, I do not hesitate to assert that I should have but one opinion about it.

FOGG: Most certainly, most certainly.

PICKWICK: Well, sir, you will permit me to assure you that I *am* a most unfortunate man, so far as this case is concerned.

DODSON: I hope you are, sir. If you are really innocent of what is laid to your charge, you really are more unfortunate than I had believed any man could possibly be. What do *you* say, Mr. Fogg?

FOGG: I say precisely what you say, Mr. Dodson.

PICKWICK: I am to understand, then, that it really is your intention to proceed with this action?

DODSON: That you certainly may.

PICKWICK: And that the damages are actually laid at fifteen hundred pounds.

DODSON: To which understanding you may add my assurance that if we could have prevailed upon our client they would have been laid at treble the amount, sir.

FOGG: Treble, without question.

PICKWICK (*angrily*): Very well, gentlemen, very well. You shall hear from my solicitor.

[*He stamps to the door, motioning to* SAM. FOGG
opens the door and bows ironically]

FOGG: We shall be very happy to do so.

[PICKWICK *stops and turns*]

PICKWICK: But before I go, gentlemen, permit me to say
that of all the disgraceful and rascally proceedings ...

DODSON (*hastily*): Stay, sir, stay.

[*He hurries to the open door and calls*]

Mr. Jackson ...

JACKSON (*who remains out of vision*): Sir?

DODSON: I merely want you to hear what this gentleman
says. (*to* PICKWICK) Pray go on, sir – disgraceful and
rascally proceedings, I think you said?

PICKWICK: I did, sir.

DODSON (*calling*): You hear that?

FOGG (*calling*): You won't forget these expressions, Mr.
Jackson?

DODSON (*to* PICKWICK): Perhaps you would care to call
us swindlers, sir. Pray do so, if you feel disposed.

PICKWICK: I do. You *are* swindlers.

DODSON: Very good. (*Calling*) You can hear, I hope, Mr.
Jackson?

JACKSON: Oh, yes, sir.

FOGG (*to* PICKWICK: You had better call us thieves, sir. Or
perhaps you would like to assault one of us. Pray do, sir,
if you would. We will not make the smallest resistance.

PICKWICK (*shaking his fists*): Why, you rascally villains?
Blackguards! You, you ...

[SAM *moves quickly in and takes his arm*]

SAM: Now, Mr. Pickwick, sir, you just come away. Battledore
and shuttlecock's a wery good game ven you an't the
shuttlecock and two lawyers the battledores, sir. Come
avay, sir. If you want to ease your mind by blowing up
somebody come outside and blow me up; but it's rayther
too expensive work to be carried out here.

[*He ushers* PICKWICK *out of the door, then comes down to the audience, as* DODSON & FOGG *leave gleefully at the other side*]

SAM: So there vos nothing for the old gen'lman to do but go to his own lawyer, which I told him he oughter done in the first place. But first he thinks he'd like a glass o brandy and warm water, just to soothe his nerves, like and your humble servant's extensive and peculiar knowledge of London vos able to guide him straight to one of them places as deals in suchlike commodities.

[*Drinkers have been drifting on and off the stage raising their pots to their lips and puffing their pipes.* PICKWICK *enters carrying a glass of brandy for himself and a mug of ale for* SAM]

PICKWICK: There you are, Sam.
SAM: Your best health, sir.
PICKWICK: And yours.

[*They drink,* SAM *nearly draining his pot without taking it from his lips. As he is doing so,* TONY WELLER *enters with a vast ale pot and a church warden pipe. He sees* SAM *and stops in surprise*]

TONY: Wy, Sammy!

[SAM *almost chokes*]

PICKWICK (*looking round*): Why, who's that, Sam?
SAM: Why, I wouldn't ha'believed it, sir. It's the old 'un.
PICKWICK: Old one? Old what one?
SAM: My father, sir. (*Approaching* TONY) How are you, my ancient?
TONY: Wy, Sammy, I han't seen you for two year and better.
SAM: No more you have, you old codger. How's stepmother?
TONY (*groans*): Wy, I'll tell you that, Sammy. There never was a nicer woman – as a widder – than that 'ere second venture o' mine. A sweet creetur, she was Sammy. All I can say on her now is that she was such

an uncommon pleasant widder, it's a great pity she ever changed her condition.

SAM (*laughing*): Is it, though?

TONY: I've done it once too often, Sammy, I've done it once too often. Take example by your father, my boy, and be wery careful o' widders all your life – specially if they've kept a public-house.

> [*He touches his forehead to* PICKWICK, *who is looking on amused*]

Beg your pardon, sir, nothin' personal, sir. I hope you ain't got a widder, sir.

PICKWICK (*laughing*): Not I.

SAM: Father, this here's Mr. Samuel Pickwick, Esquire, and I'm his vallet.

TONY: Beg your pardon, sir. I hope you've no fault to find with Sammy, sir.

PICKWICK: None whatever.

TONY: Wery glad to hear it, sir. I took a good deal o' pains with his eddication, sir.

PICKWICK: Won't you take anything with me, Mr. Weller?

TONY: You're wery good, sir. Perhaps a small glass of brandy to drink your health and success to Sammy wouldn't be amiss.

SAM: Take care, old fellow, or you'll have a touch of your old complaint, the gout.

TONY: I've found a sov'rin cure for that, Sammy.

PICKWICK (*eagerly*): A sovereign cure for the gout, Mr. Weller?

TONY: The gout, sir, is a complaint as arises from too much ease and comfort. If ever you're attacked with the gout, sir, jist you marry a widder as has got a good loud voice, with a decent notion of using it, and you'll never have the gout again. It's a capital prescription, sir, and I can warrant it to drive away any illness as is caused by too much jollity.

[*They go to the door, laughing.* PICKWICK *ushers*
TONY *out first and follows.* SAM *is just about to
exit when he remembers the audience and turns back.
He jerks his thumb in the direction of the exit*]

SAM: So then we went to see the guv'nor's lawyer, Mr.
Perker. And, of course, he tried to get Mr. Pickwick to
pay up his damages and be done vith all the fuss and
bother. *And – of course –* the old guv'nor, being what he
is, refuses point blank, though he could have paid up
ten times and never felt the pinch. 'Not a pound or a
penny of my money,' says he, 'shall find its way into the
pockets of Dodson and Fogg.' (*Sighs*) So, there's nothing
for it but to let the action come on, as it does, on the
fourteenth of Febooary, vich, as doesn't amuse the old
guvnor one bit, happens to be Walentine's Day – what
you might call a reg'lar good day for a breach o' promise
trial.

[SAM *exits. Wigged and gowned lawyers, carrying
briefs, and officials, bustle about the stage, gradually
settling down.* SERJEANT BUZFUZ *and* SER-
JEANT SNUBBIN *take seats side by side at left. A
jury of men files in and takes up solemn position to
one side of the* JUDGE'S *desk, the empty witness-
box standing at the other side near a small section
for the public, which quickly fills with men and
women,* TONY WELLER *among them.* PICK-
WICK *and* PERKER *sit side by side at the right.
The* JUDGE *enters gravely. All stand and bow. He
returns the bow, sits and takes up his quill pen.*
MRS. BARDELL, *supported by* MRS. CLUPPINS,
enters, dabbing at her eyes. They sit near counsel]

USHER: Bardell *v.* Pickwick!

[MRS. BARDELL *gives a loud, wailing sob. There
is a murmur of sympathy from the* PUBLIC *and*
JURY]

PERKER (*to* PICKWICK): Very good notion that, Mr.

Pickwick. Excellent ideas of effect, those Dodson and Fogg.

PICKWICK: Pah!

[SERJEANT BUZFUZ *rises*]

BUZFUZ: I am for the plaintiff, m'lud.

JUDGE: Who is with you, Serjeant Buzfuz?

SNUBBIN (*rising*): I appear for the defendant, my lord.

JUDGE (*writing*): Serjeant Buzfuz for the plaintiff; for the defendant, Serjeant Snubbin. Go on.

[SNUBBIN *sits down*]

BUZFUZ: May it please you, my lord, gentlemen of the jury: never, in the whole course of my professional experience; never, from the very first moment of applying myself to the study and practice of the law; never, I say, have I approached a case with feelings of such deep emotion, or with such a heavy sense of the responsibility imposed upon me. A responsibility, my lord and gentlemen, which I could never have supported were I not buoyed up and sustained by a conviction so strong that it amounts to certainty – nay, positive certainty – that the cause of truth and justice – in other words, the cause of my much-injured and oppressed client – must prevail with the high-minded and intelligent dozen of men whom I now see in the box before me.

[MRS. BARDELL *gives another loud sob.* MRS. CLUPPINS *pats her shoulder. The* PUBLIC *murmur*]

USHER: Silence!

BUZFUZ (*sentimentally*): The plaintiff, gentlemen, is a widow. Yes, a *widow*. The late Mr. Bardell, after enjoying for many years the esteem and confidence of his sovereign as one of the guardians of the royal revenues, glided almost imperceptibly from the world to seek elsewhere for that repose and peace which a customs house can never afford.

[*An impressed murmur from the* PUBLIC]

PICKWICK (*to* PERKER): Rubbish! He was knocked on the head with a quart pot in a public house cellar.

BUZFUZ: Some time before his death he had stamped his likeness upon a little boy. With this little boy, the only pledge of her departed exciseman, Mrs. Bardell shrunk from the world and to the retirement of Goswell Street. And here she placed in her front parlour window a written placard bearing this inscription, 'Apartments furnished for a single gentleman. Enquire within.' Mrs. Bardell's opinions of the opposite sex, gentlemen, were derived from a long contemplation of the inestimable qualities of her lost husband. 'Mr. Bardell,' said the widow, 'was a man of honour. Mr. Bardell was no deceiver. Mr. Bardell was once a *single gentleman* himself. Therefore, to single gentlemen I look for protection, for comfort, and for consolation. *In* single gentlemen I shall perpetually see something to remind me of what Mr. Bardell was when he first won my young and untried affections.'

MRS. BARDELL: Oh! (*A loud sob.*)

[*The* PUBLIC *murmur sympathetically*]

MRS. CLUPPINS: There, love!

BUZFUZ (*in ringing tones*): '*To* a single gentleman, then, shall my lodgings be let.' (*Lowering his voice*) And so, gentlemen, the lonely and desolate widow dried her tears, furnished her first floor, caught the innocent boy to her maternal bosom, and put the bill up in her parlour window. Did it remain there long? (*Sharply*) No! The serpent was on the watch. Before the bill had been in the parlour window three days a Being, erect upon two legs and bearing all the outward semblance of a man, and not of a monster, knocked at the door of Mrs. Bardell's house. He enquired within; he took the lodgings; and on the very next day he entered into possession of them.

(*Loudly, pointing dramatically at* PICKWICK) The man, gentlemen, was Pickwick!

[*Loud murmur*]

USHER: Silence! Silence in court!

BUZFUZ: Of this man Pickwick I will say little. I am not the man, and you, gentlemen, are not the men, to delight in the contemplation of revolting heartlessness and of systematic villainy. And when I say systematic villainy, let me tell the defendant, Pickwick, (*looking at* PICKWICK) *if* he be in court, that it would have been more becoming, in better judgment, and in better taste, if he had stopped away.

> [PICKWICK *half rises, but is pulled sharply down by* PERKER, *who wags his finger at him disapprovingly*]

I shall show you, gentlemen, that for two years Pickwick continued to reside at Mrs. Bardell's house. I shall show you that Mrs. Bardell, during the whole of that time, waited on him, attended to his comforts, looked out his linen for the washerwoman, darned, aired and prepared it for wear; and, in short, enjoyed his fullest trust and confidence. I shall show that on many occasions he gave halfpence, and even sixpences, to her little boy, and I shall prove to you that on one occasion he patted the boy on the head. I shall prove to you, gentlemen, that he distinctly offered this widow marriage, taking special care, however, that there should be no witness to their solemn contract; and I am in a situation to prove to you, on the testimony of three of his own friends, that on that morning he was discovered by them holding the plaintiff in his arms and soothing her agitation by caresses and endearments.

> [*Loud murmur. One or two cries of 'Shame!'*]

USHER: Silence in court!

BUZFUZ: Two letters have passed between these parties,

letters in the handwriting of the defendant. These letters
bespeak the character of the man. They are not open,
fervent, eloquent epistles, breathing nothing but the
language of affectionate attachment. They are covert,
sly, underhanded communications. Let me read the first.

[*He picks up a note with an expression of distaste*]

'Dear Mrs. B. – Chops and tomato sauce. Yours,
Pickwick.'

[*He tosses the note down*]

Gentlemen, what does this mean? Chops and tomato
sauce? *Yours*, Pickwick. Chops! Gracious heavens! And
tomato sauce!

[*Impressed murmur.* BUZFUZ *picks up another
note*]

The next has no date, which in itself is suspicious. 'Dear
Mrs. B., I shall not be at home till tomorrow. *Slow
coach.*' And then follows this remarkable expression:
'Don't trouble yourself about the warming pan.' The
warming pan! Why is Mrs. Bardell so earnestly en-
treated not to agitate herself about this warming pan –
unless it is a mere cover for a *hidden fire*. A mere sub-
stitute for some endearing word or promise. And what
does this allusion to the slow coach mean? For aught I
know, it may be a reference to Pickwick himself, who
has most unquestionably been a criminally slow coach
during the whole of this transaction.

[*Some laughter.* BUZFUZ *frowns*]

But enough of this, gentlemen. It is difficult to smile
with an aching heart. My client's hopes and prospects
are ruined. It is no figure of speech to say that her
occupation is gone indeed. The bill is down – but there
is no tenant. Eligible single gentlemen pass and repass
– but there is no invitation for them to enquire within.

[*His voice cracks with emotion. He produces a large
handkerchief. Ladies in the* PUBLIC *begin to cry*]

All is gloom and silence in the house; even the voice of the child is hushed; his infant sports are disregarded when his mother weeps.

> [*Loud sobs.* BUZFUZ *dabs his eyes, then blows his nose violently and suddenly resumes in ringing tones*]

But Pickwick, gentlemen! Pickwick, the ruthless destroyer of this domestic oasis in the desert of Goswell Street. Pickwick, who comes before you today with his heartless tomato sauce and warming pans. Pickwick still rears his head with unblushing effrontery and gazes without a sigh on the ruin he has made. Damages, gentlemen! Heavy damages is the only punishment with which you can visit him; the only recompense you can award to my client. And for those damages she now appeals to an enlightened, a high-minded, a conscientious, a dispassionate, a sympathizing jury of her own countrymen.

> [*There is a moment of dead silence at the end of this peroration, as* BUZFUZ *fixes the* JURY *with his stare. Then he abruptly sits down. Loud conversation breaks out. After mopping his brow* BUZFUZ *stands again*]

Call Elizabeth Cluppins.

> [*He sits again*]

USHER: Elizabeth Cluppins.

> [MRS. CLUPPINS *gives* MRS. BARDELL *a reassuring pat before leaving her seat and going to take the witness stand. The* USHER *holds the Testament up to her*]

(*Gabbling*) You swear by Almighty God that the evidence you give shall be the truth, the whole truth, and nothing but the truth?

MRS. CLUPPINS: I do.

USHER: You are Mrs. Elizabeth Cluppins?

MRS CLUPPINS: I am.

[*The* USHER *retires*]

BUZFUZ (*rising*): Mrs. Cluppins, do you recollect being in Mrs. Bardell's on one particular morning in July last when she was dusting Mr. Pickwick's parlour?

MRS. CLUPPINS: My lord and jury, I do.

BUZFUZ: What were you doing there?

MRS. CLUPPINS (*reciting lines she has obviously been taught*): I was there unbeknown to Mrs. Bardell. I had been out with a little basket to buy three pound of red kidney purtaties – (*an afterthought*) which was three pound for tuppence ha'penny – (*reciting again*) when I see – saw – Mrs. Bardell's street door on the jar.

JUDGE: On the what?

BUZFUZ: Partly open, m'lud.

JUDGE (*cunningly*): She said 'on the jar'.

BUZFUZ: It's all the same, m'lud.

JUDGE: So be it. Proceed, madam.

MRS. CLUPPINS: I walked in, just to say good morning, and went, in a permiscuous manner, upstairs and into the back room. Gentlemen, there was the sound of voices in the front room, and . . .

BUZFUZ: You listened?

MRS. CLUPPINS (*haughtily*): Beggin' your pardon, sir, I would scorn the haction. The voices were very loud and forced themselves upon my ear.

BUZFUZ: Was one of those voices Pickwick's?

MRS. CLUPPINS: It was, sir. He says, 'Mrs. Bardell, my dear,' he says, 'do you think it a much greater expense to keep two people than to keep one?'

[*With a keen glance at the* JURY, BUZFUZ *sits down abruptly.* SNUBBIN *rises*]

SNUBBIN: No questions, m'lud.

[*He sits*]

JUDGE: You may stand down, madam.

BUZFUZ (*rising*): Call Nathaniel Winkle.

[*He sits.* MRS. CLUPPINS *leaves the stand and returns to* MRS. BARDELL, *who presses her hand affectionately*]

USHER: Nathaniel Winkle!

[WINKLE *enters nervously, gives* PICKWICK *a little bow, and takes the stand. The* USHER *approaches with the Testament*]
[*The words are so gabbled as to be indistinguishable*]

Swear Almighty God truth, whole truth, nothing but truth.

WINKLE: Y-yes.

USHER (*almost inaudibly*): 'thaniel Winkle.

WINKLE: Yes.

JUDGE: Winkle? What's your Christian name, sir?

WINKLE: N-Nathaniel, sir.

JUDGE (*writing*): Daniel. Any other name?

WINKLE: Nathaniel, sir – I mean, my lord.

JUDGE: Nathaniel Daniel, or Daniel Nathaniel?

WINKLE: Nathaniel, my lord, only Nathaniel. Not Daniel at all.

JUDGE: What did you tell me it was Daniel for, then?

WINKLE: I d-didn't, my lord.

JUDGE: You did, sir. How could I have got Daniel on my notes, unless you told me so?

BUZFUZ (*rising*): Mr. Winkle has a short memory, m'lud. We shall find means to refresh it before we have quite done with him, I dare say. Now, Mr. Winkle, attend to me, if you please. I believe you are a particular friend of Pickwick, the defendant?

WINKLE: I have n-known Mr. P-Pickwick now, as well as I recollect, nearly . . .

BUZFUZ (*interrupting*): Pray, Mr. Winkle, do not evade the question.

WINKLE: I was j-just ab-bout to say . . .

BUZFUZ: Will you, or will you not, answer the question?

WINKLE: Y-yes, I am.

BUZFUZ: Yes, you are. And why couldn't you say that at once, eh, sir? Perhaps you know the plaintiff too?

WINKLE: I don't know her. I've seen her.

BUZFUZ: Oh, you don't know her, but you've seen her. How often have you seen her, sir?

WINKLE: I ...

BUZFUZ: A hundred times?

WINKLE: I ...

BUZFUZ: Fifty?

WINKLE: S-s-s ...

BUZFUZ: Seventy-five times, then. Now, sir, do you remember calling on the defendant Pickwick at these apartments in Goswell Street on one particular morning in the month of July last?

WINKLE: I do.

BUZFUZ: Were you accompanied by a friend of the name of Tupman, and another of the name of Snodgrass?

WINKLE: I was.

BUZFUZ: Then, sir, tell the gentlemen of the jury what you saw on entering the defendant's room on this particular morning.

WINKLE: The ... the ... the ...

BUZFUZ: Out with it, sir.

WINKLE (*with a rush*): The defendant, Mr. Pickwick, was holding the plaintiff in his arms, with his hands clasping her waist, and the plaintiff appeared to have fainted away.
[*Court murmur*]

BUZFUZ (*carefully*): Did you hear the defendant say anything?

WINKLE: I heard him c-call Mrs. Bardell a g-good creature, and I heard him ask her to compose herself, for what a situation it should be if anybody should come – or words to that effect.

BUZFUZ: Now, Mr. Winkle, listen to me carefully. Will you

undertake to swear that Pickwick did not say on this occasion, 'My dear Mrs. Bardell, you're a good creature; compose yourself *to this situation*, for to *this situation* you must come'?

WINKLE: I was outside, and c-couldn't hear distinctly.

BUZFUZ (*pouncing*): You were outside and didn't distinctly hear. Then can you swear that Mr. Pickwick *did not* make use of the expressions I have quoted?

WINKLE (*miserably*): No, I cannot.

BUZFUZ: That will be all, sir.

[*He sits down dramatically. Loud murmur*]

USHER: Silence!

SNUBBIN (*rising*): Mr. Winkle, I believe that Mr. Pickwick is not a young man?

WINKLE: Oh, no. He's old enough to be my father.

SNUBBIN: Had you ever any reason to suppose that he was about to be married?

WINKLE: Oh, no.

SNUBBIN: Did you ever see anything in Mr. Pickwick's manner and conduct towards the opposite sex to induce you to believe that he ever contemplated matrimony?

WINKLE: Oh, *no*!

SNUBBIN: Has his behaviour, when females have been in the case, always been that of a man who, having attained a pretty advanced period of life, content with his own occupation and amusements, treats them only as a father might his daughters?

WINKLE (*confident now*): Not the least doubt of it.

SNUBBIN (*pleased*): You have never known anything in his behaviour towards Mrs. Bardell, or any other female, in the least degree suspicious.

WINKLE: No, no. (*With a laugh*) Except one trifling occasion, which, I have no doubt, might be easily explained ...

SNUBBIN (*hastily*): Thank you, Mr. Winkle, that is all.

[*He sits down hurriedly.* WINKLE *is about to*

leave the box, but BUZFUZ *rises and holds up his hand*]

BUZFUZ: Stay, Mr. Winkle, stay! Will your lordship have the goodness to ask him what this one instance of suspicious behaviour towards females, on the part of the gentleman who is old enough to be his father, was?

JUDGE: You hear what the learned counsel says, sir.

WINKLE: M-my l-lord . . .

JUDGE: You must answer.

WINKLE (*wretchedly*) It . . . was when he was f-found in a lady's sleeping compartment . . .

['*Oh!*' *from* SPECTATORS]

. . . It was at Ips-s-swich. The m-m-magistrate s-s-said . . . (*bursting out*) But it was all a mistake, my lord!

SNUBBIN (*rising; severely*): You may leave the box, sir.

[WINKLE *almost runs off the stage*]

BUZFUZ (*rising*): Call Samuel Weller.

[*He sits*]

USHER: Samuel Weller!

[SAM *enters and takes the box. The* USHER *waves the Testament at him*]

Almight truth whole truth nothing but.

SAM: I do, sir.

JUDGE: Name?

SAM: Sam Weller, my lord.

JUDGE: Do you spell it with a V or a W?

SAM: That depends upon the taste and fancy of the speller, my lord. I never had occasion to spell it more than once or twice in my life, but I spells it vith a V.

TONY WELLER: Quite right too, Samivell, quite right. Put it down a we, my lord, put it down a we.

JUDGE: Who is that who dares address the court?

SAM: I rayther suspect it was my father, my lord.

JUDGE: Do you see him here now?

SAM (*looking deliberately everywhere except at the public*): No I don't, my lord.

JUDGE: If you could have pointed him out I would have committed him instantly. Proceed, Serjeant Buzfuz.

BUZFUZ (*rising*): M'lud. Now, Mr. Weller.

SAM: Now, sir.

BUZFUZ: I believe you are in the service of Pickwick, the defendant in this case.

SAM: I am in the service of that 'ere gen'lman, and a wery good service it is.

BUZFUZ (*jocular*): Little to do and plenty to get, I suppose.

SAM: Oh, quite enough to get, sir, as the soldier said ven they ordered him three hundred and fifty lashes.

JUDGE: You must not tell us what the soldier or any other man said, sir. It's not evidence.

BUZFUZ: Do you recollect anything particular happening on the morning when you were first engaged by the defendant?

SAM: I had a reg'lar new fit out o' clothes that morning, gen'lmen of the jury, and that's all.

BUZFUZ: Do you mean to tell me, Mr. Weller, that you saw nothing of this fainting on the part of the plaintiff in the arms of the defendant?

SAM: Certainly not. I was in the passage till they called me up, and then the old lady was not there.

BUZFUZ (*sarcastically*): You were in the passage and yet saw nothing. Have you a pair of eyes, Mr. Weller?

SAM: I have, sir, and that's just it. If they wos a pair o' patent double million magnifyin' gas microscopes of hextra power, p'raps I might be able to see through a flight o' stairs and a door. But bein' only eyes, my wision's limited.

[*loud laughter in Court*]

USHER (*laughing*): Silence! Silence in court!

BUZFUZ (*put out*): It's perfectly useless, my lord, attempting to get any evidence through the impenetrable stupidity of this witness. Stand down, sir.

SAM: Would any other gen'lman like to ask me anythin'?

> [*More laughter.* SAM *stands down and comes to the audience. Behind him in dumb show we see* BUZFUZ *orating to the Court; then* SNUBBIN]

(*To audience*) Well, Serjeant Buzfuz went on and on, and it didn't take half an eye to see that the poor old guv'nor was going to be done for. Those letters alone could've done the trick. When Buzfuz proved to the Court how men sometimes call their wives 'Duck', and then pointed out that a man who was fond of chops and tomato sauce might use them as a term of haffection instead, there wasn't a juryman who didn't nod.

> [SNUBBIN *sits down.* SAM *steps aside to watch as the* JURY *confer amongst themselves and the* FOREMAN *stands*]

USHER: Gentlemen of the jury, are you all agreed upon your verdict?

FOREMAN: We are.

USHER: Do you find for the plaintiff or for the defendant?

FOREMAN: For the plaintiff.

USHER: With what damages?

FOREMAN: Seven hundred and fifty pounds.

> [*Members of the* PUBLIC *shake their fists at* PICKWICK, *with shouts of* 'Serve him right!' 'Not enough!' 'Old brute!', *and so forth.* MRS. BARDELL *and* MRS. CLUPPINS *embrace. The* JUDGE *rises and all follow suit. He bows and exits, followed by all except* PICKWICK, PERKER *and* SAM]

PICKWICK: Well, Perker, they imagine they will get costs also, I suppose.

PERKER: Probably, Mr. Pickwick, my dear sir.

PICKWICK: Then attend to me, Perker. Messrs. Dodson and

Fogg may try, and try, and try again. But not one farthing of costs or damages shall they ever get from me, if I spend the rest of my existence in a debtor's prison.

> [*He sweeps off the stage, followed by* PERKER, *protesting*]

PERKER: But my dear sir, my dear sir ...!

SAM (*to audience*): And nothing Mr. Perker or 'is friends could say would make the hemperor change 'is mind. And so we found ourselves, him and me, in the Fleet, a miserable sort o' place where those as never wants to work finds it easy just sittin' round all day, and those as is always a-vorkin' when they can gets wery low by bein' boxed up. (*Shaking his head*) It's no sort of place for any decent man, let alone the master, who wasn't used to such sights.

> [PICKWICK *enters*]

But could I tell him so?

PICKWICK: Sam ...

SAM: Well, sir.

PICKWICK: I have felt from the first that this is not the place to bring a young man to.

> [SAM *gives the audience a glance, as if this confirms what he has just been saying*]

SAM: No, sir. Nor an old 'un, neither.

PICKWICK: You're quite right, Sam. But old men may come here through their own heedlessness, and young men may be brought here by the selfishness of those they serve. It is better for those young men that they should not remain here. Do you understand me, Sam?

SAM (*firmly*): No, sir. I do *not*.

PICKWICK: Try, Sam, try.

SAM: Vell, sir, I think I see your drift; and if I do see your drift, it's my 'pinion that you're a comin' it a great deal too strong, as the mailcoachman said to the snowstorm when it overtook him.

PICKWICK: I see you do comprehend me, Sam. Independ-
　　ently of my wish that you should not be idling about a
　　place like this for years to come, I feel that for a debtor
　　in the Fleet to be attended by his manservant is a
　　monstrous absurdity. For a time, Sam, you must leave
　　me.

SAM (*sarcastically*): Oh, for a time, eh, sir?

PICKWICK: Yes, for the time that I remain here. Your
　　wages I shall continue to pay. And if I ever do leave this
　　place, Sam – *if* I do – I pledge you my word that you
　　shall return to me instantly.

SAM: Now *I*'ll tell *you* wot it is, sir. This here sort o' thing
　　won't do at all, so don't let's hear no more about it.

PICKWICK: I am serious and resolved, Sam.
　　　　　　　　[*He exits briskly*]

SAM (*to audience*): Vell, now, there vos a perwerse old
　　gen'lman for you! But it takes more than that to put the
　　likes of me out, as the fire said ven the lady spit in it.
　　D'you know the Insolvent Court in Lincoln's Inn
　　Fields? There's more unvoshed skins there at any time
　　than all the pumps and shaving shops between Tyburn
　　and Whitechapel could tend to between sunrise and
　　sunset.
　　　　　　[TONY WELLER *strolls on from opposite*]
　　Vot a place for your humble servant to go to!
　　　　　　　　[SAM *sees his father*]

TONY: Samivel! Vot *are* you a doin' of here?

SAM: Vot about you, old 'un?

TONY: A fren' o' mine, as drives the Dover stage, is 'avin' 'is
　　pertition for discharge under the Hact, and I come
　　along vith 'im. But Samivell, if you're 'ere for your
　　guv'nor you're a-wastin' your time and his. They won't
　　pass that werdict over, Sammy.

SAM: Who said anything about the werdict? By the vay,
　　'ow's stepmother?

TONY (*brightening*): Wery queer. I think she's a-injurin'
herself gradivally vith too much o' that 'ere pineapple
rum and other strong medicines o' the same natur'.
There's hope for me yet, Samivell.

SAM: Ah, vell! Now, old codger, just open them ears o' yourn
to this affair o' mine. This perwerse Pickwick 'as turned
me out o' the Fleet and reckons 'e's a-goin' to stay there
by 'imself till 'e dies of it, rayther than pay up.

TONY: Wot! Stop there by hisself, without nobody to take
his part! Why, they'll eat him up alive, Sammy.

SAM: That's about the strength of it. Now, don't you see any
vay of us takin' care on him?

[TONY *scratches his head copiously, then brightens*]

TONY: A pianner, Samivel. A pianner!

SAM: Wot?

TONY: A pianner forty, as your guv'nor can have on hire in
there. Vun as won't play, Sammy.

SAM: And wot 'ud be the good o' that?

TONY: Let him send out for them to come and fetch it back
because it ain't no use to 'im. Are you awake now?

SAM: No.

TONY: There ain't no *vurks* in it. It'll hold him easy, vith
his hat and shoes on, and breathe through the legs, vich
is holler. Have a passage ready for him to 'Merriker.
The Merrikin gov'ment will never give him up, ven they
find as he's got money to spend. Let the guv'nor stop
there till Mrs. Bardell's dead, or Mr. Dodson and Fogg's
hung (which last ewent I think is the most likely to happen
first, Sammy), and then let him come back and write a
book about the 'Merrikins as'll pay all his expenses and
more, if he blows 'em up enough.

SAM (*staggered*): Cor!

TONY: Eh? Vot, Samivell?

SAM: *Cor!*

TONY: It's no use, Samivell?

[SAM *shakes his head silently*]

Vell, then, 'ow about gettin' him out in a turn-up bedstead? Or dressin' 'im up like an old 'ooman with a green wail?

[SAM's *head continues to shake*]

Then it's no thoroughfare, Sammy. No thoroughfare.

SAM: Well, then, I'll tell you vot it is. I'll trouble you for the loan of five-and-twenty pound.

TONY: Wot! Wot good'll that do?

SAM: P'raps you may ask for it back five minutes arterwards. P'raps I may say I von't pay. Now, you von't think o' arrestin' your own son for the money and sendin' 'im off to the Fleet, *vill* you, you unnat'ral vagabone?

[TONY *stares for a moment, then begins to chuckle, nudging* SAM *in the ribs. They laugh together.* TONY *rummages in his clothes and produces bank-notes*]

TONY: 'Ere you are; and I know a gen'lman 'ere as'll do the business for us in no time. A limb of the law, Sammy, as has got brains, like the frogs, dispersed all over 'is body and reachin' to the wery tips of his fingers. A friend o' the Lord Chancellor, Sammy, who'd only have to tell him what he wanted and he'd lock you up for life, if that wos all.

SAM: I say, none o' that!

TONY: Sssh! 'Ere 'e comes.

[SOLOMON PELL *enters and comes up to* TONY]

PELL: Well, sir, your friend stands third on the opposed list, and I should think it would be his turn in about half an hour. I don't like to boast, sir – it's not my way – but I can't help saying that if your friend hadn't been fortunate enough to fall into my hands ... Mm, I remember once dining with the late Lord Chancellor. There was only two of us, but everything as splendid as if twenty people had been expected – the great seal on a dumb-waiter at his right hand, and a man in a suit of armour guarding the mace with a drawn sword – when he said to me, 'Pell, no false delicacy, Pell, but you're a man of talent. You can get anybody through the insolvent court, and your country should be proud of you.' Those were his very words. 'My lord,' I said, 'you flatter me.' 'Pell,' he said, 'if I do, I'm damned.'

TONY (*clearing his throat*): Mr. Pell, you're the wery gen'lman as I might ha' wanted to see this minute.

PELL: Oh?

TONY: Yes, and it's like this 'ere. This vagabone son o' mine 'as borrowed twenty-five pound and 'e won't pay a farden back. Now, son o' mine 'e may be, but twenty-five pound is twenty-five pound, and if you was to show me a haffidavit for debt, then I sh'd swear to it as fast as winkin'.

PELL: Mr. Weller, be so good as to step this way. The matter is as good as settled.

> [PELL *ushers* TONY *off*, TONY *turning unseen by him to bestow a huge wink upon* SAM]

SAM (*to the audience*): So here's your humble servant, back in the Fleet and not to be shifted. But I wonder how the old guv'nor's a-goin' to take it?

> [*He glances round, then puts his finger to his lips for silence.* PICKWICK *enters, reading a book*]

PICKWICK: Ah, Sam, my good lad. I'm delighted to see you. I had no intention of hurting your feelings, my faithful fellow. Just let me explain at a little more length why I do not wish you to remain here with me.

SAM: Won't presently do, sir?

PICKWICK: Certainly. But why not now?

SAM: 'Cos I've a little business to do as I'd better see arter at once.

PICKWICK: Business? In here?

SAM: Yes, I've got to see arter my bed.

PICKWICK: *Your* bed?

SAM: Yes, sir, for now I'm a pris'ner, like your good self, sir. Arrested this arternoon, and the villain as put me in 'ull never let me out till you go yourself.

PICKWICK: B-bless my heart and soul!

SAM: Just what I says, sir.

PICKWICK: But this is preposterous, Sam. How much is your debt?

SAM: Twenty-five pound, sir.

PICKWICK: As little as that! Then it's quite simple: I shall pay it for you.

SAM: Thankee kindly, sir, but that ain't no use. He's a bad-disposed, spiteful, windictive creetur, with a hard heart as there ain't no softenin'. No, sir, I'd rayther not ask a favour of this here remorseful enemy.

PICKWICK: It's no favour, asking him to take his money!

SAM: Beg pardon, sir, but it 'ud be a wery great favour to pay it, and he don't deserve none. No, sir, you takes your determination to stay here on principle, and I takes mine on the same ground. And there's an end to it, sir.

> [*The* COBBLER *staggers on stage and slowly collapses, to lie still.* SAM *and* PICKWICK *hurry to him and raise his head*]

SAM: This poor fellow's dyin', sir.

PICKWICK: Ah, I fear you're right. Nothing to be done for him, poor wretch.

> [*The* COBBLER *groans and opens his eyes*]

COBBLER: Open . . . window.

SAM (*to* PICKWICK): There ain't no window in here, sir.

COBBLER: No . . . air. This place . . . pollutes it. Was air, fresh, few years ago . . . but grows hot, heavy, within these walls. Can't . . . can't breathe it.

PICKWICK: Have you been here long?

COBBLER: Twelve . . . years. Chancery suit. Lawyers had

all my money, years ago. In here for a thousand ...
stop here till I die ...

PICKWICK: Sam, this poor devil has been slowly murdered
by the law for twelve years.

SAM: Aye, sir.

COBBLER: I hope ...

PICKWICK: Yes? Tell me your wish?

COBBLER: Hope my merciful Judge will bear in mind
heavy punishment on earth. Twelve years in this grave.
Child died, and could not even kiss him in ... in little
coffin. May ... may God forgive me. (*Very weakly*) He
... has seen my solitary, lingering death.

> [*His head falls back.* SAM *lays him down*]

SAM: He's got his discharge now, sir.

PICKWICK (*rising*): I have seen enough, Sam. My head
aches with the scenes I have witnessed. Henceforward
I will be a prisoner in my own room.

> [PICKWICK *exits.* SAM *beckons off stage.* TWO
> PRISONERS *come in and carry off the* COBBLER.
> PERKER *comes rushing on, looking round*]

PERKER: Ah, Sam, there you are!

SAM: Good day, Mr. Perker, sir. What brings you a-wisitin'?

PERKER: I'd, er, like a word with your master, Sam. As
soon as possible.

SAM: Wery vell, sir. I'll fetch him.

PERKER: Sam, Mrs. Bardell has been brought into this very
prison.

SAM: Brought into the Fleet, sir!

PERKER: In execution of her costs. She had entered into an
undertaking for the amount after the trial, and since Mr.
Pickwick has refused to pay, Dodson and Fogg have
taken *her* in execution. By Jove, they're the cleverest
scamps I ever had anything to do with.

SAM (*slyly*): It, er, wouldn't, like, be you wot suggested it to
'em, would it, sir?

PERKER (*with mock indignation*): I ...? Sam, how dare ...
>   [SAM *begins to laugh heartily.* PICKWICK *enters*]

PICKWICK: How dare he do what, Perker? Sam, control yourself this instant!

SAM: Beg pardon, sir.

PERKER: Er, Mr. Pickwick, I wished to have a word with you *re*, er, Bardell and Pickwick.

PICKWICK: Now, Perker, I distinctly told you that I did not wish to ...

PERKER: You don't like to hear the case named, eh?

PICKWICK: No, I do not.

PERKER: Sorry for that, for it will form the subject of our conversation.

PICKWICK: Now ...!

PERKER (*overriding him*): Now, sir, Mrs. Bardell, the plaintiff in the action, is within these walls, on the suit of Dodson and Fogg. Since they have been unable to recover their costs from you, they have proceeded against her.

PICKWICK: The ... scoundrels!

PERKER: Quite so. Well, my dear sir, the first question I have to ask is, whether this woman is to remain here?

PICKWICK: How can you ask me that? It rests with Dodson and Fogg.

PERKER: It does not rest with Dodson and Fogg, my dear sir. It rests solely, wholly and entirely with you.

PICKWICK: With me?

PERKER: I say, my dear sir, that no one but you can rescue her from this den of wretchedness; and that you can only do that by paying the costs of this suit into the hands of Dodson and Fogg.
>   [PICKWICK *raves speechlessly*]

SAM: Don't take on so, sir.

PERKER: I have seen the woman this morning. By paying the costs you can obtain a full release for her and a discharge from the damages for you, as well as a volun-

tary statement from her hand that this business was,
from the very first, fomented and encouraged and
brought about by these men, Dodson and Fogg. She
deeply regrets ever having been the instrument of
annoyance or injury to you, and she entreats me to
intercede with you and implore your pardon.

[PICKWICK *is about to protest, but* PERKER
forestalls him]

You now have an opportunity, my dear sir, of placing
yourself in a much higher position than you ever could
by remaining here, which would only be imputed – by
people who didn't know you, of course – to sheer,
dogged, wrong-headed, brutal obstinacy.

PICKWICK: Now, Perker, really!

PERKER: Can you hesitate to take that opportunity when it
restores you to your friends, your old pursuits, your
health and amusement? When it liberates your faithful
and attached servant, whom you otherwise doom to
imprisonment for the whole of your life? And, above all,
when it enables you to take the very magnanimous
revenge of releasing this woman from a place of misery
and debauchery to which no *man* should ever be con-
signed, if I had my will, but the infliction of which on
any woman is even more frightful and barbarous?

PICKWICK (*after a slight hesitation*): Perker, my friend, you
are right.

[*They clasp hands.* TUPMAN, SNODGRASS *and*
WINKLE *enter*]

TUPMAN:
SNODGRASS: } Pickwick!
WINKLE:

PICKWICK (*shaking hands in turn*): Snodgrass! Tupman!
Winkle, my dear fellow!

WINKLE: P-p-p-pickwick. H-how do you do?

PICKWICK: I do very well, thank you.

TUPMAN: Pickwick, in short the matter's this. We've come here to beg you to desist from this absurd defiance and release yourself.

SNODGRASS: Yes, sir. Our hope is that what no consideration for yourself will induce you to do, a regard for the happiness of your friends might.

WINKLE: Abs-s-solutely. The P-pickwick Club has been in adjournment t-too l-long.

SAM: Hear, hear, gen'lmen!

PERKER: You hear, my dear sir?

PICKWICK: Perker – pay them.

ALL: Bravo!

PICKWICK: Sam.

SAM: Sir?

PICKWICK: As to your own liabilities, I suspect you will not find it difficult to get your discharge from them?

SAM: Vell, sir, as it just so happens, I 'spect it could be managed.

[*The others laugh*]

PICKWICK: Depend upon it, gentlemen, I was resolved to remain here on a point of principle. Now, I have been amply shown that principle may over-stretch itself into perversity. With all my heart I am ready to leave – but I vow never to forget the plight of the poor wretches I leave behind in this vile place. May the day soon come when imprisonment for debt shall cease and it shall no longer be possible to forget that in such vile places live fellow creatures who, but for the grace of God, might have been ourselves.

OTHERS: Hear, hear!

PICKWICK (*brightening*): So Sam ...

SAM: Aye, sir?

PICKWICK: Purchase five-and-twenty gallons of mild porter and have it distributed amongst my fellow inmates.

SAM: *Aye,* sir.

PICKWICK: And enquire about a coach to take us home.

SAM: I vill, sir. And I vish the horses had been three months
and more in the Fleet, sir.

PICKWICK: Why, Sam?

SAM: Vy, sir? A-cause how they'd go, if they had ha' been.

> [*The curtain falls on general laughter and hand-
> shaking amongst the friends*]